Forensic Handwriting Examination

Forensic Handwriting Examination
A Definitive Guide

by

Reed C. Hayes, CDE

Reedwrite Press
Honolulu, HI

Library of Congress Cataloging-in-Publication Data

Hayes, Reed C.
Forensic Handwriting Examination: A Definitive Guide /
Reed C. Hayes

p. cm.
Includes bibliographic references and index.
ISBN 0-9778415-0-2
1. Handwriting—Identification. 2. Legal Documents—Identification.
I. Hayes, Reed C. II. Title.
2026

This book contains material from various sources highly regarded in the document examination field. A variety of references are listed. Reasonable effort has been made to present reliable data and information, however the author cannot assume responsibility for the validity of all materials contained herein or for the consequences of their use.

Direct all inquiries to Reed Hayes, P.O. Box 235213, Honolulu, Hawaii, 96823.

Trademark Notice: Product or corporate names may be trademarks or registered trademarks, and are used solely for identification, instruction or explanation, without intent to infringe.

Dedication

To the memory of my brother Richard Hayes and sisters
Elaine Jordan, Jeanette McPherson & Edith Leavitt
and to my brother Lester Hayes

The Author

Reed Hayes operates a handwriting and document examination business in Honolulu, Hawai'i. He has studied handwriting for nearly five decades, and has worked internationally on projects including the book and video production of *The Diary of Jack the Ripper* and the book *Alexander Cartwright: The Life Behind the Baseball Legend.* He has also examined and rendered opinions on the questioned will of Queen Lili'uokalani, Hawaii's last reigning monarch.

Mr. Hayes is a graduate of the Andrew Bradley Training Course in Forensic Document Examination (beginning and advanced) and holds certification from the National Association of Document Examiners (2001), with re-certifications in 2006, 2011, 2016, 2021 and 2026. He is a member of the American Handwriting Analysis Foundation and serves as a board member of the National Association of Document Examiners and the Scientific Association of Forensic Examiners.

Mr. Hayes is the author and co-author of several books, including *Between the Lines, Danger Between the Lines* and *Reflections of a Forensic Handwriting Expert.* He currently teaches a distance course in forensic handwriting and document examination and has instructed students from around the globe. He has presented numerous seminars and workshops about handwriting throughout the U.S. and has been a guest speaker at the British Institute of Graphologists and the Association of Qualified Graphologists in London.

In addition to anything handwriting related, his personal interests include genealogical research.

Acknowledgments

Special thanks are extended to the following people: Debbie Jenae for carefully scrutinizing the manuscript for grammatical and spelling errors; Richard Kokochak for providing a thorough critique of the first draft and making sound suggestions for improvement; Kathie Koppenhaver for clarifying some of the information, offering advice and correcting technical issues; and Sheila Lowe for reading the manuscript and pointing out errors and possible misconceptions. I am grateful for the combined efforts of these people which have helped lift the book to a higher level.

Contents

Preface

Forensic handwriting examination involves the analysis of handwritten material in an effort to verify or determine authorship, detect forgery and prove or disprove authenticity.

Handwriting examiners are called upon to scrutinize signatures, written or handprinted text, initials or numbering on various personal and business documentation with the intent of proving origin, authorship or genuineness. They also investigate graffiti and anonymous writing, usually with the intent of identifying the writer. In many instances their findings are presented in courts of law to assist the judge and/or jury in understanding technical evidence about which they possess special knowledge and experience.

Handwriting is a highly complex act involving the writer's individual neuromuscular makeup. It is largely dependent upon habitual movements and letter shapes that conform to each person's own master pattern which is firmly entrenched in memory. Yet its execution is influenced by both internal and external factors such as health, ingestion of drugs or medication, heightened emotional response, and writing circumstances. Further, because people do not perform exact, repetitive movements of any type, each person has a certain amount of natural variation in his or her writing which must be considered in the analysis.

Although one of the oldest forensic disciplines, handwriting examination is not an exact science. Unlike identification of an individual through DNA which relies on solid data, handwriting is subject to variables which prevent it from being strictly quantified. (However, certain aspects of writing can be measured as demonstrated in this book.) The handwriting expert relies on the examination of material to reach opinions in much the same manner as a physician who considers various tests, patient symptoms and prior medical history in diagnosing illness. Each works with facts and evidence to arrive at conclusions according to his or her knowledge, training and experience with similar cases.

While the evaluation of handwriting is to a certain extent subjective according to each examiner's skill level and experience, it is nevertheless based on axioms, principles and theories which have been utilized and relied upon by handwriting experts for decades. Handwriting examination adheres to the scientific approach of observation, measurement, explanation and verification.

Every spurious handwriting case is unique due to the nature of the question involved, the writing under investigation and the writing collected for comparison purposes. The effective examiner reviews each case logically and objectively in an effort to get at the truth as evidenced in the handwriting and documentation presented for the exam. They consider every possibility according to the matter and materials at hand, and deduce the most solid conclusions possible based on what is derived from the available writing and documentation.

Forensic examination of handwriting is not a straight-forward task that follows exact methods, although a standard approach is normally taken by most examiners when working cases. Given the myriad of possible writing features which vary from one person to another, as well as within an individual's own writing and according to the prevailing circumstances under which the writing was produced, it becomes challenging to present a system of analysis which will work the same in every instance.

With that challenge in mind, the objective of this text is to act as a guide in the examination process. It is meant to provide an understanding of handwriting examination principles and techniques based on years of experience reviewing handwriting and documentation of all types. It follows a more or less systematic approach and all attempts have been made to present the material in a practical, useful manner, given the complexity of writing and the examination process. It is offered as a reference source for serious students of forensic handwriting examination as well as those who are already proficient in the discipline.

This book is not intended to replace other handwriting examination texts, many of which are referenced herein. It is not meant to be a comprehensive treatise on such a vast subject about which others have written so extensively.

As suggested, this book features the investigation and analysis of handwriting, which includes handprinting and signatures. Little material is presented with regard to other document examination concerns such as the nature of papers, inks and writing implements. It does not detail the examination of typewritten and computer generated text, nor does it cover use of techniques such as detection of indentions and document alterations like erasures. It does not describe document photography, ultraviolet and infrared lighting or special laboratory equipment, all information available in standard document examination texts.

Despite today's reliance on computers and other technological advancements for communication, the complexities of handwriting will always exist in varying degrees, as will the conditions and circumstances under which writing is produced. However, the examiner's knowledge and skill with respect to evaluating handwriting must continue to grow with ongoing study and the experience gained from working numerous and diverse cases.

Much of the information contained in this book is not new. However, the material presented springs from years of experience pondering the intricacies of writing for one reason or another. It is my intention that the text will help educate and stimulate the reader in this fascinating, complex field.

Reed C. Hayes
Honolulu, Hawaii 2026

1. Introduction to Handwriting Examination

Forensic handwriting examination involves the evaluation and analysis of handwritten or handprinted material on various types of documentation for the purpose of detecting forgery, identifying writers and proving or disproving authenticity.

What are Handwriting and Document Examiners?

A handwriting examiner is one who is qualified to review handwriting or signatures for forensic purposes. Handwriting examiners, also known as forensic handwriting analysts or handwriting experts, authenticate writing and verify authorship of documents and signatures. They evaluate anonymous notes, graffiti or any other handwritten matter that may be under question as to origin or authorship. They are often called upon to investigate alleged forgeries.

While most handwriting experts also consider other document features besides writing, some are not qualified or do not have the proper equipment to do so.

Those who do have the necessary qualifications are referred to as document examiners, questioned document experts or forensic document examiners. They critically examine the physical nature of a document in every way possible to determine its authenticity in its entirety and in every aspect and part. This generally includes a study of any writing on the document.

Questioned document examiners borrow from numerous disciplines and sciences in formulating their opinions and may be called upon to determine a number of facts about a document in question aside from the writing. Other document features such as paper punch holes, stains, folds, watermarks, paper type or ink might be at issue.

The scope of both handwriting and document examiners' work is to determine the truthfulness and legality of documents by way of their physical attributes. This book focuses primarily on the handwriting examiner's role in this regard and how he or she can successfully work questioned writing cases.

What Are Handwriting Analysts?

Contrary to general belief, forensic handwriting examiners are differentiated from handwriting analysts who evaluate writing for the purpose of determining character or personality. Although both measure, study and analyze essentially the same components of handwriting, they do so for different purposes. Usually the handwriting analyst works with the writing of a known person to determine that individual's character. The forensic expert generally works with unknown writing with the intent of proving authorship or establishing identity, often for legal purposes.

Forensic handwriting examiners sometimes get their start in the discipline by first studying graphology (the generic term for character analysis by handwriting) or Graphoanalysis™ (a specific method of handwriting analysis). Training in graphology familiarizes them with the intricacies of the writing process and the various ways in which handwriting factors can be produced by different writers.

A graphology background will therefore most certainly benefit the forensic writing examiner, but it is nevertheless imperative that training in the forensic discipline be obtained before attempting to render opinions regarding questioned writing matters. In some instances graphologists have improperly presented themselves to their clients and the court as forensic handwriting examiners when in fact they are not qualified in that arena.

On a few occasions Graphoanalysts have rendered courtroom testimony as to an individual's state of mind at the time of having written or signed a document, or whether something was written under duress. However, given the long-standing, rather unfair association of graphology with fortune telling, courts generally frown on the reliability of character assessment of writing and usually do not permit testimony in that regard.

Forensic writing examiners who have also studied graphology or Graphoanalysis™ must keep the two disciplines separate. Character evaluations are not acceptable as part of forensic handwriting reports and will surely be challenged as unfounded by an opposing attorney.

What is an Expert Witness?

In many cases, once an opinion or opinions have been reached, the handwriting examiner will be called as an expert witness to demonstrate those findings in a legal setting such as a deposition, hearing or a courtroom trial, perhaps before a jury.

Until the examiner is actually called to testify, he or she is technically a consultant. Once subpoenaed for deposition or required by the client or a judge to appear at a formal hearing or trial, the examiner becomes a witness.

By definition an expert witness is a person who possesses special skills or knowledge acquired by way of training or experience not normally possessed by the layman, and is therefore permitted to draw conclusions or express opinions that are otherwise inadmissible in testimony.

To appear as an expert in a court proceeding, a witness may be qualified by knowledge, skill, experience, training or education. As an expert one need not have complete knowledge of his or her field of expertise. However, he or she must be well versed in every aspect of the problem at hand. For example, if the chemical nature of ink is part of the question, the examiner needs to know about the relevant chemistry and be able to perform such tests as thin layer chromatography.

Every time an expert appears at a trial, the judge handling that particular case must qualify him by considering his expertise. The examiner will be questioned about training, education, credentials and experience. If the examiner measures up to the requirements and it appears that the intended testimony will be helpful to the matter at hand, the judge will qualify the expert and allow testimony in that particular case.

What are Documents?

Within the meaning of the standard rules of evidence, a document is any physical embodiment of information or ideas such as a letter, contract, receipt, deed, diary, journal or agreement, to name but a very few. In a legal setting documents may also be referred to as instruments.

According to *Black's Law Dictionary*[1], a document is an instrument on which is recorded lettering, figures or marks of which the original, official or legal form may be used evidentially.

The term document applies to instruments bearing writings, words or figures that are printed, photocopied, scanned, faxed, microfilmed or photographed. There are original documents, photocopies, faxes or

1. Henry Campbell Black, *Black's Law Dictionary*, St. Paul, MN: West Publishing Company, 1983.

electronic scans of original documents, computer generated documents and, of course, forged documents.

In a legal sense, documents are utilized to prove facts such as rights, identity, ownership, entitlement, agreement and financial obligations. Documents such as letters, notes and memos are utilized to communicate information. Documents like checks, vouchers, money orders and the like are obviously used to transmit money. In a very loose sense, a wall bearing graffiti or even a body on which a note is written could be considered a document of sorts.

What is Forgery?

Black's Law Dictionary defines forgery as the false making or material altering, with intent to defraud, of any document or writing which, if genuine, might apparently be of legal efficacy or the foundation of a legal liability.

More simply, forgery is the falsification of an instrument or document so that it may be presented as genuine. With forgery there is always an intent to deceive or defraud. Often the intent behind forgery is financial or material gain.

Forgery generally involves the falsification of handwriting or signatures, but may also involve the alteration of a document's import or features, such as the removal, addition or substitution of information (e.g., check raising, changing of contract information, substitution of entire pages of documents). In any case, forgery is passing off a document as genuine when in fact it has been falsified.

With respect to handwriting or signatures, there are basically three types of forgery: 1) simulation (an attempt to make a freehand imitation of the writing or signature), 2) simple forgery (no intent to mimic the signature, but simply write the name) and 3) tracing.

Forgeries can also be created by the "cut and paste" method where a genuine signature is lifted from a valid document (either mechanically or electronically) and placed onto a new, false document. With today's technology, it is relatively easy to create an entirely new "original" document bearing anyone's signature or altering a document's meaning or import.

Signing an assumed or fictitious name to a document, as in the case of identity theft, is also considered forgery, again because the perpetrator is doing so with the intent to defraud. Another type of forgery is signing the name of a non-existent person, entity or corporation.

Obtaining one's signature by force, coercion or trickery also constitutes forgery. An example of this would be when a new will or other seemingly legal document is created and then placed in front of an incapacitated elderly person for signature. The victim is led to believe they are signing a valid instrument or a document that will be to their benefit. Obviously, detecting fraud in this instance would be difficult because the signature on the new, false document is technically authentic.

It should be noted that genuine duplicate signatures are possible due to use of rubber stamps. The autopen, sometimes used by prominent people who are required to sign massive amounts of documentation, produces numerous identical signatures. These signatures, although not handwritten, would also be considered genuine.

What Types of Documents are Forged?

Any kind of documentation is subject to forgery—wills, codicils, deeds, contracts, checks, agreements, school records, charge slips, guest checks at restaurants, tax returns and other personal, legal or financial documents.

Forgeries are usually committed for the purpose of material gain, but can also be cover-ups for both legal and illegal acts. Such forgeries might include falsified business or professional records (especially those of a financial nature as in hiding embezzlement or misappropriation of funds), altered inventory records to cover employee theft, or doctored medical records to hide evidence of malpractice.

Even children can be forgers. It is not uncommon for a truant child to show up at school the following day with a note from mother, written and signed in a clumsy, childish script.

Potential Clients

Handwriting examiners' potential clients include anyone who has access to or involvement with written documentation whose genuineness is suspect.

For example, John Doe claims that his father's will has been falsified by another family member and he seeks assistance in proving who bilked him out of his inheritance. Or his name has been illegally signed in a credit card transaction and he wants professional proof that it's not his signature. Or his signature has been forged on a contract, or his insurance application has been falsely initialed which changes his coverage, or he has received threatening or maligning letters and is seeking identification of the perpetrator.

Likely clients will include attorneys representing individuals who claim they did or did not sign some document, financial institutions (banks, credit card companies, credit unions), insurance companies and police departments (although most have their own in-house experts). From time to time the examiner may receive inquiries from confused or possibly even crazed people who are crying forgery as part of a conspiracy against them.

Possible handwriting related cases include:

• Suspect signatures, always in an attempt to identify or eliminate the writer and, if found to be non-genuine, usually to determine who authored the writing.

• Suspect document, but with an apparently genuine signature. (Just because a signature on a document is authentic does not mean that everything else about the document is.) Which part, if any, of the text above the signature has been tampered with?

• Family disputes, often after someone's death.

• Divorce or post-divorce issues such as an ex-spouse accused of signing tax returns for the other.

• Disputes over land ownership or inheritance.

• Anonymous notes or letters—usually in a disguised or imitated style and generally meant to cause harm to the recipient.

• Graffiti—often on schoolroom walls with disparaging comments about teachers, sometimes in lavatory stalls with sexual connotations or otherwise derogatory remarks about management or fellow employees.

• Medical malpractice cases—Have a physician's records been altered after the fact to show that he is not negligent for a patient's improper care? Insertion of single words or medical abbreviations may come into play, or the sequence of various entries, the type of pen used, or which page was on top of which when writing was produced.

• Consultant cases—The examiner may be called upon to simply review another expert's work and render clues as to effective cross-examination questions.

2. Reviewing the Entire Document

Most document examination cases involve the analysis of signatures or handwriting. However, in order to reach completely accurate opinions, examiners must be aware of document features other than the handwriting.

Prominent handwriting and document examiner Ordway Hilton, author of Scientific Examination of Questioned Documents, wrote that "the examination of a questioned document is a detailed analysis of the whole, of all its elements, prominent and minute. The final opinion is an evaluated summation of the findings of these separate studies." [1]

While not all documents contain disputed features aside from signatures, in order to properly examine a document, the possibility of a problem involving other than the signature should be considered. All documents should be examined in their entirety to determine if there are any red flags that merit further investigation. Often there is a valid explanation for any problem encountered, but in some cases the problem may be supportive to findings of non-genuineness.

Features of the document other than handwritten material may reveal pertinent information aside from whether the signature is authentic. For example:

- The purported signature date may not match the situation (a document signed and dated after the purported signer was deceased).
- Information on the document may have been removed or replaced.
- Indentations in the signature line area might reveal tracing.
- More than one pen was used on the original.
- Pages have been substituted.

Nowadays it is relatively easy to digitally alter various features of documents or create new ones in their entirety. Sometimes questioned documents contain signatures that have been "lifted" from the original and placed onto the suspect document. By examining and comparing originals of all the known material available, it may be possible to discover the source of such cut-and-paste signatures. Although a signature may be deemed authentic, its placement on the document in question

1. Ordway Hilton, "The Whole Document," International Journal of Forensic Document Examiners, Vol. 2, Number 2, April/June 1996, Shunderson Communications, Ontario, Canada.

could bc spurious. This of course underlines the importance of reviewing original material whenever possible.

It is far better for the document examiner to perform a detailed analysis of a document in order to uncover any hidden problems before his or her opinions are challenged by an opposing examiner who has discovered a document flaw that has gone undetected by the first examiner. Also, the client may want to simply use the examiner's opinion to support that the signature is authentic, when it is in fact genuine, but the document itself is fraudulent. Given this scenario, a thorough examination of the document as a whole might prevent the misuse of the examiner's services. [2]

Original documents are always preferred, but in many cases examiners work only from photocopies, sometimes because originals have somehow "disappeared" or are conveniently or legitimately lost. Although accurate conclusions can be reached based on copied material, in cases where originals are unavailable any opinions rendered should be qualified, considering that there are some features of writing and documentation that are not discernible in photocopies.

When originals are available, the practiced document examiner will consider every aspect of the document. Even with copies, care should be taken to review the document in its entirety if for no other reason than to determine its continuity and appropriateness. This can be accomplished by establishing an examination protocol by following the considerations listed below.

Generally, the examiner should be alert to such features as the overall condition of the document (whether soiled, wet or peculiar in any way); the paper's suitability for the occasion; the style, history and character of the handwriting; the kind, model and history of any typewritten or computer generated material; the type, class and likely age of ink; the form and composition of the printed matter; and evidence contained on the envelope or any accompanying or related documentation.

The astute document expert will attempt to answer the following questions pertaining to various document features:

- What type of paper was used to create the document? Is it appropriate for the occasion?
- Was the company in existence at the time of the letterhead? Was it

2. Edna Robertson, *Fundamentals of Document Examination*, Chicago: Nelson-Hall Publishers, 1991.

located at the address in the letterhead on that date?

• If it contains a zip code, were zip codes in existence at that time and is it correct?

• Are there other indications of the document's age such as printer's marks on forms?

• Was the person still living on the date the document was purportedly signed? Was he or she physically capable of signing the document?

• If the paper is irregular in size, has it been cut or trimmed to eliminate other information?

• If there are obliterations or erasures, what information has been obliterated or removed? If correction fluid has been used, what has been covered?

• If more than one handwriting is present on the document, who is (are) the other people who wrote on the document?

• If the questioned document is a pre-printed form, was the form manufactured prior to the date on the document?

• Is there unusual arrangement of material on the page or gaps in spacing? If so, does it appear to have been created from other documents?

• If a check, is the date in sequence with other checks written before or after it? Does the endorsement match the writing on the face of the check?

• If it is a copy, is the original available and if not, why not? Does it appear to be a first generation or multi-generational copy?

• If witnessed, are all the witnesses' signatures verifiable and authentic?

• If notarized, are the notary's signature and stamp authentic? Is the notary's log book available for inspection? If the signature in question is in fact authentic, the signature in the notary log should also be authentic.

• If there is other writing on the document in addition to the signature, does the writing belong to the person who allegedly signed the document?

• With entries that purport to be continuous, are the dates in sequence? Have any entries been crowded into a space?

• When misspelled words are present, are they significant? Does the suspect make similar errors in his or her normal writing?

• If the documentation is soiled, crumpled or creased, is its condition consistent with the reported age or storage of the document or is it possible that the document has been artificially aged to match its date?

• If a document is folded, does any writing cross a fold? If so, was the writing done before the paper was folded, or after?

• Are any pencil marks, carbon lines or impressions present on or near the signature line to indicate a tracing?

• If embossing or impressions are evident, is there a pressure pattern on the back of any other document to indicate that it might have been used as a model for tracing? Does any other signature (known or in question) appear to be an exact duplicate of the questioned signature?

• If the writing on a document is tremulous, is tremor also present in the comparison standards of the same approximate time period? Does the tremor appear genuine or simulated?

• Is all the ink on the document in the same color? Does it appear that the same pen was used throughout?

Multiple Page Documents

When documents consist of more than one page, there is added potential for problems regarding authenticity. If the entire document is in fact one unit, each page must be like the others in all physical details, unless there is a valid reason for any inconsistencies.

After reviewing a multiple page document for the points given above, the examiner should also consider the following:

• Is there evidence that suggests a page has been inserted or deleted? Has one or more pages been substituted?

• Do all pages have consistent margins, numbers, alignment and paper?

• If the document has been folded, do the folds on each page match the others?

• Does the content flow from one page to the next or does a page appear to be missing?

• Does all typewritten or computer generated material on each page match? Was the same font used throughout?

• Is the same handwriting or initials found throughout the entire document?

• Was the same pen utilized throughout?

• If each page bears initials, were all written by the same pen, or by the pen of each person who wrote on the document?

• Are all pages of the same paper or from the same box or tablet?

• Have the pages been bound together only once or the same number of times? How? By staples or paper clips? Was the document bound in its present form when executed or have pages been substituted?

• Are there writing impressions from a previous page or from some other source?

• Are all of the signatures on the document authentic, those of the principal signer(s) as well as those of any witnesses or notaries public?

Any document may bear its own special problems and each must be recognized and then determined to be consistent—or inconsistent—with authenticity. The conscientious document examiner should consider and evaluate all evidence available to ensure that the final opinion reflects a detailed analysis of the entire document. By examining more that just the writing on a document, authenticity or fraud can more accurately be determined.

3. The Basis of Handwriting Examination

In discussing the basis for handwriting comparison it is important to consider how writing develops. Essentially, one's handwriting goes through four stages throughout life: the formative stage, the impressionable or adolescent stage, the mature stage and the stage of degeneration.

During the formative stage, which commences in the early grades of school, handwriting development begins, usually with manuscript (printing) and gradually advancing to cursive where individual letters are joined together. Methods of instruction and writing models of course vary from one region to another, although the learning process is primarily the same.

When first learning to write, children construct letters slowly and deliberately as they commit individual shapes to memory and associate them with sounds. Essentially they imitate what is presented in the handwriting model. Depending on innate skill, memory, development of eye-hand coordination and other factors, each pupil gradually evolves toward graphic maturity at which time fully developed skill and experience are reflected in movements of the pen.

No matter how thorough or well intentioned the writing instructor, no student is capable of recreating exactly what is recommended by the copybook style. His or her writing slowly takes on its own characteristics due to temperament, personal tastes and capabilities, and flair for individuality.

Children from the same classroom will necessarily have some commonalities in their handwriting as a result of having studied the same model, but as their skills and personalities evolve, so will their writing. In addition to individual letter shapes, other features of the writing such as spacing, arrangement and letter proportions will collectively become the products of that child and that child alone.

It is to be noted that more mentally advanced children with active imaginations are sometimes the poorest writers. Not surprisingly, those who are talented at drawing are often considered good writers due to their imitative skills.

In today's technologically advanced world where the use of computer keyboards is generally more frequent than using pen and paper, handwriting instruction is not given as much importance as it was in years gone by. Other culprits are the rejection of repetitive drills as a teaching tool and government testing that determines a school's worth based on other subjects like reading and math.

Students are no longer required to practice writing movements for hours at a time, and are often given free rein with regard to handwriting style. In many school districts cursive writing is a mere afterthought to manuscript. Such inattention to writing instruction and less emphasis on following strict penmanship rules leads to opportunities for even more individualized handwriting which, as a result, is potentially more readily identifiable.

It is not uncommon to consciously or unconsciously introduce new or varied features into one's writing over time, perhaps the result of imitation or personal taste. During the impressionable stage the adolescent may toy with new handwriting features, often copied from the writing of family members or some admired person. By the time a student graduates from high school, his or her writing characteristics are usually more or less stabilized and the writing begins to enter the mature stage. However, the attainment of graphic maturity varies from one individual to another and it appears that the impressionable stage may be lengthening due to lack of frequent handwriting practice so prevalent in today's educational system.

Graphic maturity is reached when all handwriting movements are made from habituated neuromuscular patterns.[1] Mature writing is recognized primarily through the high skill level of the writing along with fluency in changes of direction, spontaneous movement, good rhythm, consistent strokes and a smooth baseline. Letter shapes are uniform and may deviate from copybook forms. At this point the writer demonstrates control of the entire process and the writing has become a well developed habit.

Writing naturally changes over time according to maturity, lifestyle, and personal and occupational experiences. Physical injuries or disabilities, either temporary or permanent, can also affect one's writing, as might trauma. And, as one declines physically with age, the handwriting will decline as well (the stage of degeneration). These possibilities underscore the importance of relying upon contemporaneous writing

1. Katherine Koppenhaver, "The Road to Graphic Maturity," Journal of the National Association of Document Examiners, Vol. 24, No. 1, Summer 2001.

samples when working questioned handwriting cases.

Despite the evolution of one's writing, it nevertheless maintains certain permanent characteristics and identifying features that are often quite inconspicuous, usually even to the writer himself. Signatures often remain especially individualistic over an extended time frame.

Considering the complexity of the writing process and the unique neurological, psychological, emotional and physical makeup of each human being, the probability that two people will have identical writing without individually unique features is practically nil.

While this is so, the handwriting examination process is nevertheless quite complex. Every writing examination requires careful scrutiny of all features and cannot be approached mechanically. As humans are living, breathing beings with internal impulses and reactions to external stimuli, it is nearly impossible for anyone to write identically the same from one sitting to the next. Except in very rare cases it is unlikely that two passages of writing from the same individual will be so much alike that there is no variability between them. Even a well practiced writer using his or her favorite writing tool, writing under the same circumstances and for the same purpose, will produce two sets of writing that are different in at least some respects.

Because no two genuine writings are replicas of one another, the handwriting examiner must call upon sound judgment to determine if any of the dissimilarities present are due to natural variation or different writers. Minus any fundamental differences that cannot be reasonably accounted for, the sum total of the similarities in letter construction and detail can only be explained as being of common authorship.

Handwriting Examination and the Scientific Method

While handwriting examination is based on scientific methods and follows certain principles and axioms, opinions are partly subjective due to variables which potentially affect the writing process. The accurate and successful handwriting examiner gains expertise from extensive training and experience. Combined with a sense of logic and careful consideration of certain principles related to the act of writing, this aids in the correct evaluation of any variables present.

Although many of its components are measurable, handwriting is not purely quantifiable. Therefore, handwriting examination is considered a discipline or, as determined by the court in US vs. Starzecpyzel, 93 CR 553, a technical skill rather than an exact science.

Handwriting examiner Richard Kokochak has said that when we speak of exact science we speak of absolutes in which any conclusions we reach cannot possibly be wrong. A test for this is to ask if it is possible for two reasonable people using scientific methods to disagree with the results. If they could, the science they are using is not exact.

Just as in the field of medicine where diagnoses are based on evaluation of scientific tests and patient data, handwriting opinions are also based on scientific principles, measurements and astute observation. In either case, it is the specialist who interprets the findings and renders opinions therefrom.

It can be argued that, like doctors, handwriting examiners follow sound logic and scientific reasoning. After all, if the process were simply a matter of counting up similarities and differences, then every forgery would pass as genuine and every disguised writing would pass as the product of a different writer.[2]

In forensic handwriting evaluation, the significance of points of similarity or difference can vary depending on the circumstances. Huber and Headrick write that "Handwriting, being what it is, may never permit precise determinations to be made of the value or significance of any particular writing characteristic or the probability of occurrence level for any combination of characteristics."[3] However, they continue, educated approximations can be made which are sufficiently reliable for identification purposes.

Without empirical data such as that which supports the hard sciences, handwriting examiners must basically resort to their knowledge and experience in determining the importance of each bit of handwriting information. In like manner, the judge or jury hearing a case takes into account various pieces of evidence, each having its own importance as a factor in the overall scheme of things. Consequently, assigning significance to each factor is subjective and will be based on each person's education, training and experience.

To help ensure reliability of opinions, it is imperative that hand-

---

2. Andrew Bradley, Advanced Studies: Extended Training in Document Problems, Denver, CO: Andrew Bradley and Associates, 1993.

3. Roy A. Huber and A. M. Headrick, *Handwriting Identification: Facts and Fundamentals*, New York: CRC Press, 1999.

writing examiners follow, wherever possible, consistent procedures in handling their cases. Each matter is of course unique to a certain extent—questioned signatures will be handled differently than anonymous notes—but consistency in each category is important in order to avoid inadvertent errors. The examination protocol presented in Chapter 9 should prove helpful in this respect.

Principles and Theories of Writing Identification

Handwriting examination is scientific in the respect that it is a branch of accumulated and accepted knowledge founded on theories, general truths and principles that have been discovered through study, experimentation and research.

The complexity of the handwriting identification process does not fit well with simple formulas and exact procedures, especially considering the variables associated with the writing process and the circumstances surrounding the production of writing.

However, certain principles can be relied upon in reaching logical conclusions. Some of those principles are presented here, although it must be noted that this is not an exhaustive list on such an extensive topic.

1. No two persons are exactly alike in action, speech or handwriting.
2. Each person has distinct handwriting characteristics which distinguish his or her writing from that of every other person.
3. An individual's normal writing always has some degree of natural variation (even though in some instances it might be barely perceptible) which prevents writing from being mechanically exact.
4. No person can assume all of another's complex and inconspicuous writing habits in order to successfully reproduce them in an extended writing sample.
5. When a writing has been imitated (simulated) it will necessarily bear similarities to the model that is being copied.
6. When a person attempts to imitate another's signature or writing, the imitator must necessarily eliminate many if not all personal writing characteristics.
7. A person who has imitated or traced another's signature can rarely be identified from characteristics in the imitated or traced signature. However, this will depend on the amount and type of comparison ma-

terial available.

8. In a disputed handwriting comparison, one distinctive element alone seldom justifies a definite conclusion.

9. To prove that two writings were produced by one person, similarities must exist between them which cannot be attributed to coincidence or accident, and there can be no fundamental unexplainable differences.

10. To prove that two writings were not produced by the same person, fundamental disparities must exist between them which cannot be accounted for by coincidence, accident, disguise, psychological influence or physiological factors.

11. The more frequent and unusual the accumulation of mutually confirming qualities and personal writing habits, the more certain can the writer be identified.

12. The quality of the written line is directly related to movement and will therefore be altered if there is any disruption to mind, muscles and/or nerves.

13. There is no scientific way of proving the reason for any disruption in one's usual writing.

14. Physical age cannot be reliably determined from handwriting. Gender can sometimes be deduced, but not with absolute certainty.

15. Every person has unconscious writing features and habits which, when written naturally or spontaneously, act as identifiers. These features cannot be entirely suppressed, except in limited amounts of text or writing.

16. Handwriting is subject to change throughout the course of a person's life from childhood scribbles to mature writing in adulthood to cramped or poorly controlled writing of old age or infirmity.

17. A person's writing can be influenced by health, medications and drugs, injury, physical condition and abnormal emotional or mental states.

18. No one can write better or more fluently than his or her very best.

19. A person cannot write a disguised or otherwise unnatural hand as effortlessly as when using his or her natural handwriting.

20. Attempts at disguise are usually not successful due to the person's inability to totally eliminate subconscious or automatic writing habits.

21. It is possible to consciously distort one's writing so that it becomes unrecognizable.

22. Attempted disguise produces writing that is of inferior quality.

23. A writer cannot exclude personal discriminating writing features if he is not aware of them, nor can one assume those features of another's writing if he is not cognizant of them.

24. Handprinting and numbers bear individual characteristics which make them as identifiable as handwritten material.

25. With few exceptions, handwriting cannot be successfully compared to handprinting. Signatures can only be successfully compared to other signatures, not to other writing.

26. If two signatures or passages of writing are identical, one of them must necessarily be a digital, electronic or photocopied reproduction of the other.

4. Primary Handwriting Features

In the handwriting comparison process the examiner looks first to the more apparent writing features such as class characteristics and arrangement for any immediate signs of possible inauthenticity. He or she then works step-by-step through the less obvious characteristics, comparing them for differences and similarities. Measurements are made, idiosyncratic letters and formations are examined and finally, after considering certain writing complexities as explained in the following chapter, conclusions are reached as to authorship.

As an aid to objectivity and to avoid overlooking any handwriting feature that might be significant to the immediate task, it is suggested that the examiner follow the same essential process with each questioned handwriting. Worksheets presented later in this book can be helpful in this regard.

Considering each of the characteristics discussed in this chapter will assist in reaching an accurate, successful outcome. However, while the material presented here may be used as a guide in the examination process, any findings and observations must be considered critically and with an eye toward logic given the nature and circumstances of the case at hand.

The examiner should remember that in identifying or eliminating writers it is the cumulative evidence of all handwriting features which is forceful and compelling.

Class Characteristics

Class characteristics are those aspects or elements of writing that situate a person within a group of writers, or that give written communication a group identity.

People who learn from the same handwriting model will necessarily have some writing elements in common, and individuals who share nationality will also have some handwriting similarities. It is safe to assume that two pupils from the same classroom will have at least a few similar writing characteristics, but a person educated in Micronesia, for example, will have a different writing style than someone from Montana, barring the remote possibility that they were taught the same handwriting model.

Certain professionals (such as engineers and accountants) often have handwriting characteristics in common, as do family members, nuns from a particular order or blind people taught to write using a specific template.

Class (or style) characteristics are sometimes seen in the handwritings of social or school groups—teenagers who adopt writing fads, or gang members who utilize signs and symbols unique to their group. Often writing styles reflect the era from whence they came, such as copperplate writing of the Victorian era, more recent Palmer handwriting, or the "puffy" lettering style of the 1960s and 1970s that appeared on advertising, record album covers, posters and in school girl diaries.

Common copybook styles in the United States include the Palmer method, D'Nealian script and Zaner-Bloser writing, the latter of which is still quite popular with educators. Italic calligraphy is another handwriting model popular in many school systems today. Class characteristics of these and other writing systems include specified letter forms, size, slant and proportion.

Fig. 4.1—Zaner-Bloser Handwriting Model

However, despite attempts by the teacher of any handwriting model to instruct students in exact letter construction, no pupil is able to completely follow the prescribed formations. Each develops individualized handwriting shapes, movements and inconspicuous features which distinguish their writing from that of fellow students. The overall style of a student's writing will likely follow the model closely enough that the pictorial effect may be similar to that of a classmate's handwriting, but unique features will identify the writer, particularly as graphic maturity is reached.

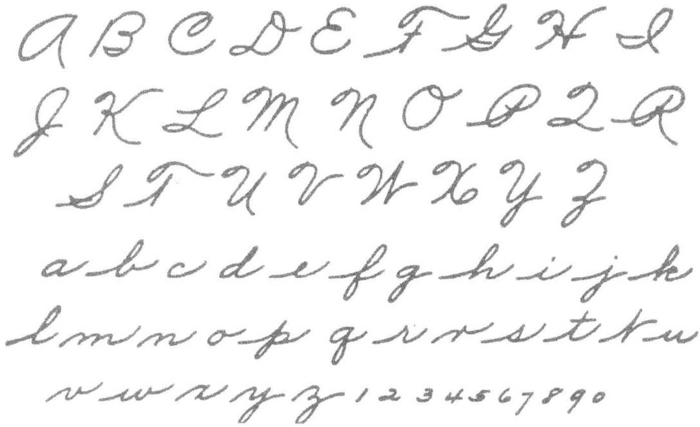

Fig. 4.2—Palmer Handwriting Model

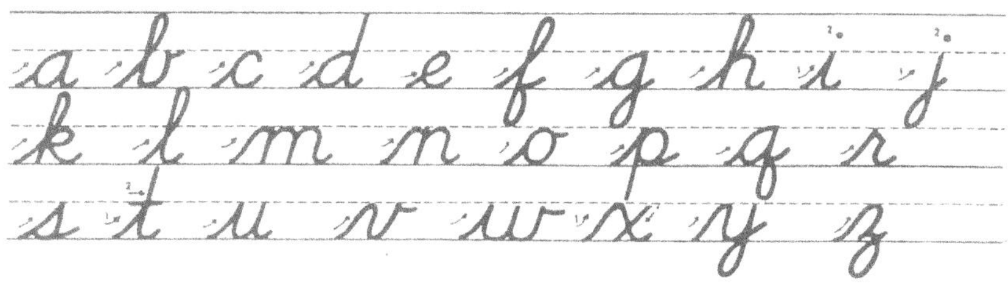

Fig. 4.3—D'Nealian Handwriting Model

As handwriting instruction currently receives generally less emphasis in the education process, it is less likely that students from the same class today will develop the degree of similarity with each others' writing than pupils did in days gone by when good handwriting was considered an honorable accomplishment. Ultimately, less stringent writing instruction and more individual freedom will tend to make the handwriting examiner's task of identification or elimination easier.

While class characteristics may serve to connect a writer to a particular group and therefore narrow the list of suspects to a certain extent, they are rather ineffective as identifying features. The examiner must therefore consider what lies beyond the immediately apparent, focusing on less obvious characteristics of the writing such as idiosyncratic formations, spacing, letter proportions, connections and pressure patterns.

Pictorial Appearance

The pictorial appearance of the writing is the first thing that strikes one's eye. It is the initial impression that makes an individual's writing recognizable by friends and family.

The pictorial quality of writing is governed by such factors as slant, size, arrangement, spacing and the degree of simplification or elaboration, all of which together give the handwriting a certain "look." This may be the result of instruction in a particular writing model. The examiner must of course delve beyond any initial impressions and scrutinize the more inconspicuous features of the script before reaching conclusions as to authorship.

It is possible for handwritings produced by different people to initially appear similar, but upon closer examination it will be found (based on the underlying inconspicuous features) that in fact they are of uncommon authorship. On the other hand, given the effect of natural variation, it is also possible for writings from the same person to have little in common upon first glance. Again, the initial impression is based on the pictorial quality and that impression may be proven inaccurate by more thorough examination.

For a simulated signature to pass as genuine, that signature must have qualities in common with the signature that is being copied. It must look authentic or it will immediately be questioned. The forger normally makes a concerted effort to write or sign like the victim, but is usually unable to master the less obvious qualities of the known writing while suppressing his or her own writing characteristics.

In short, it is risky to rely solely on the pictorial effect of the writing to determine authenticity.

Arrangement

Arrangement refers to the placement of the writing on the page or writing surface. It is the overall layout which includes the relationship of the writing to the edges of the page, the division and construction of paragraphs and the manner in which the writing is positioned on the paper. Arrangement is characterized by the white space on the page and, at the same time, the portion of the paper occupied by the writing.

As a general rule, writing arrangement reflects habitual characteristics, particularly in writing not related to business transactions. Business-related documents—correspondence or memos written in the scope of employment—are more likely to follow an established system or the formatting typical of the company for whom the writer works, although even in that instance individual arrangement features are often evident. Correspondence or writing produced for personal reasons is apt to be more individualized where arrangement is concerned.

The examiner should note whether the arrangement of material on the page or envelope is in any way abnormal or unusual. Especially wide gaps between the text and signatures or any other arrangement oddity are important considerations.

Margins

Habits of creating margins vary from person to person. Some write with exceptionally narrow margins, while others leave wider spaces between the writing and the edge of the page. The top margin might be wide and the bottom narrow or vice-versa. The left margin may remain relatively consistent from top to bottom, or drift inward. There is a fair amount of conscious control over the left margin, although it may be governed to a certain extent by any printed rule on the left side of the page. The right margin tends to afford more freedom and is less dependent upon conscious choices, except perhaps when and how words are hyphenated.

Paragraph construction

Paragraph construction is taught in school but few people follow prescribed indentation and spacing recommendations. Writers form their own habits in this regard which are rarely abandoned even in disguise attempts. Any unusual manner of indenting, positioning or spacing of paragraphs are indicative of individual writing habits and therefore useful in identification.

Writing on envelopes

Arrangement of written material is highly revealing on envelopes where each person is free to develop a unique style. Placement of the return and delivery addresses with respect to the edges of the envelope are significant, as is spacing between lines. Even if the writer makes a careful attempt at disguise, arrangement patterns are usually overlooked, frequently with respect to envelopes and often on the letters they contain. In anonymous letter cases the layout of envelope writing can be especially valuable.

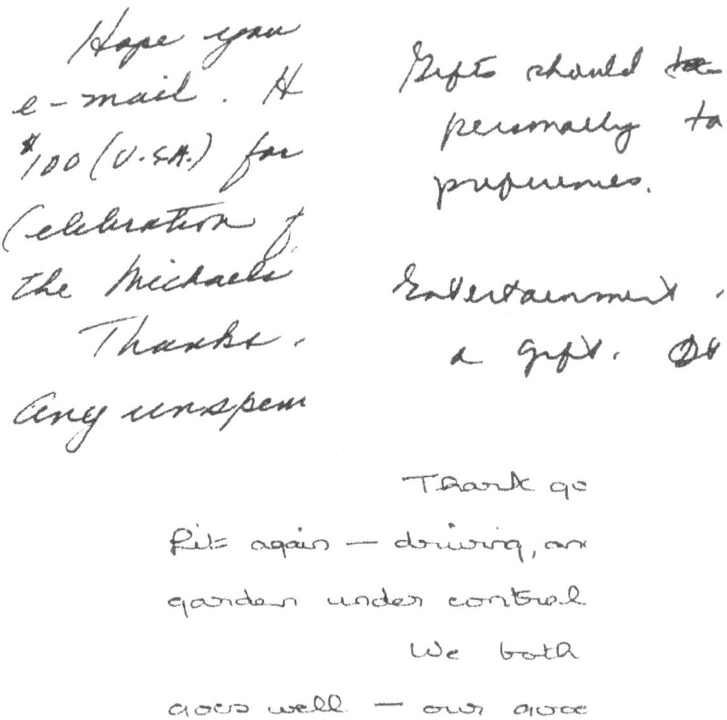

Fig. 4.4—Paragraph habits

Alignment

Alignment is the positioning of letters, words and sentences in relation to the real or imagined baseline of writing. The baseline is the line upon which we write. We start to write by positioning the pen or pencil at a point relative to this line. We then move away from this point in creating a stroke or series of strokes that form the first letter. By doing so we have established a base for the first letter and those letters that will follow.

While as students we are instructed to place our handwriting on straight lines, each of us has developed individual alignment habits. Some are capable of writing relatively consistent lines, while others create wandering or even erratic lines across the page. Entire lines of writing may slope upward or downward, or may begin to move upward and then descend toward the end. Sometimes lines of writing will begin to droop just at the end.

To some extent alignment can be influenced by circumstances such as awkward or unusual writing positions. Writing with a paper held on one's lap may cause the lines to follow a convex pattern, for example. Attempting to change the slant of one's script from forward to vertical or backhand will often cause the writing lines or individual words to drift upward.

Armed with various and sufficient comparison samples, the examiner should look for any alignment patterns that remain consistent from one known writing to another. Some writers always place their writing above the baseline, while others drop below the line. In some cases, individual letters or words are aligned in a particular way. If the same letter is continually misaligned in the same fashion, that would be considered an individual characteristic of the writer. Specific words can also show alignment habits, as when writers opt to write the word "and" on an upward or downward slope. (See Figure 4.5.)

Alignment is significant in the evaluation of signatures, particularly if the examiner is provided with sufficient known samples written under various conditions so as to determine the writer's usual alignment habits. As with handwritten text, when a person signs a document the signature may adhere to the line, ride above it or cut through it. There may be specific letters or formations of the signature that are placed uniquely with respect to the line. The distance from the beginning of the line and where the person begins signing may also be an identifying factor. When no printed line is available for the signature, the examiner should still look carefully at the alignment on the imaginary baseline.

Although line direction can be significant in the examination process, minor deviation in this respect may be nothing more than normal variation or the result of some condition at the time of writing. In some cases (as with writing greeting cards) the person may purposefully write with upward-slanted lines to create an effect, but not do so when writing for other purposes. Ultimately, the frequency of alignment features demonstrated in numerous writing samples will be the determining factor as to whether they are products of habit or altered temporarily by the circumstances at hand.

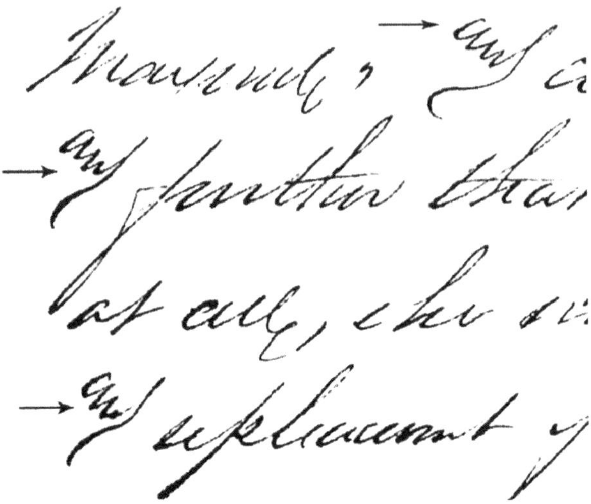

Fig. 4.5—Individualized word alignment

Size and Proportion

Handwriting size is a learned habit which reflects the range of movement of one's fingers and hand. There is individuality in this regard with some writers producing exceptionally small or even microscopic script, while others have very large writing.

In this context, three sizes will be discussed: primary, absolute and relative. Three handwriting zones or areas will also be referred to: midzone, upper zone and lower zone.

Measurements are made with respect to the midzone of the writing, the area containing the small letters that rest on the baseline. The upper zone contains upper loops and upward extensions from the midzone. The lower zone consists of the lower loops and any downward extenders from the midzone.

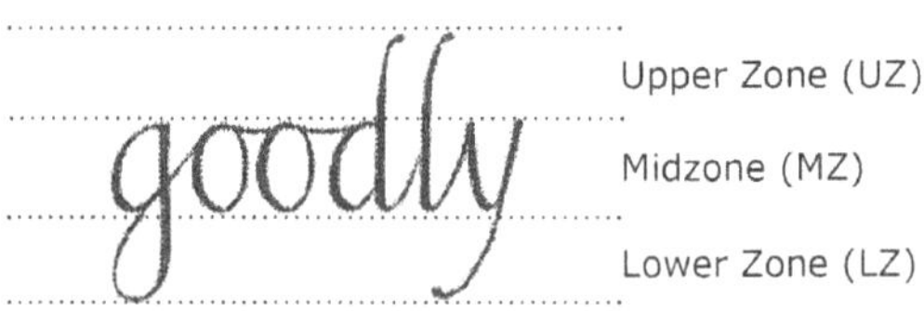

Fig. 4.6—The three zones of handwriting

Primary writing size is the average height of the midzone. Absolute writing size is the distance between the top of the upper zone and the bottom of the lower zone.

Relative size is the height of each of the three zones in relationship to one other. These ratios are especially reliable in handwriting examination because they are generally consistent from one writing session to another. Also, when working with machine copied material there may be uncertainty as to the exact size of the original writing, but the ratios will remain unaltered whether the document has been reduced or enlarged.

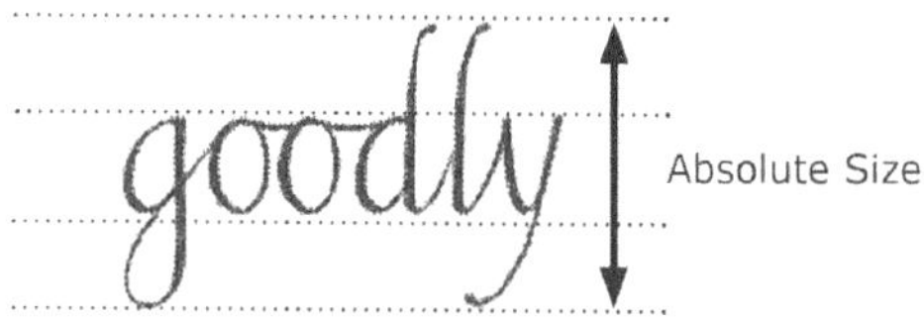

Fig. 4.7—Absolute size of writing

Starting with the height of the upper zone and progressing downward, the size ratio of the three zones is expressed as UZ:MZ:LZ. Most copybook ratios are 1:1:1 as illustrated in Figure 4.6, but the ratio or proportion is often individualized and therefore useful in the identification process.

If, for instance, the upper zone height (UZ) is 4mm, the midzone height (MZ) is 3mm and the lower zone lengths (LZ) measure 6mm, the measurements would be expressed as follows:

UZ :	MZ :	LZ
4 :	3:	6

To calculate the ratio of the three zones, the MZ is divided by the other two zones; the UZ is divided by the MZ and the LZ is also divided by the MZ. In the instance noted immediately above, the resulting ratio is 1.3 : 1 : 2.

Letter proportions remain relatively constant despite any deliberate or unconscious change in the primary or absolute size of the writing. Writing with a wider pen point than usual will most often result in larger writing overall, but letter proportions will nevertheless remain. Using a pen with a finer point than normal may cause the writing to diminish in overall size but, again, ratios will not change appreciably.

Ratios are also difficult to disguise, even if the person thinks to do so. Deliberately changing the size of one of the writing zones may prove successful, but when two or more zones are altered, the writing will surely display poor rhythm due to disruption of the writer's usual habits pertaining to proportions.

Klara Roman measured the size of several thousand school children's handwritings and found that by the time a child is 12 years old, letter height is fairly well established. However, the ratio of upper and lower loops is not yet stable, and the lower zone size is especially subject to change until the child attains writing maturity.[1]

It is not uncommon for upper or lower zone extenders to vary in size or formation within an individual's writing, making it important to determine the writer's individual pattern of variation in that regard. Measurement of such upper or lower zone extensions in a writing sample would entail calculating their respective averages. The examiner should also note whether one particular letter is consistently of a different size than similar letters, e.g. the letter h normally taller than the letter l. Such a pattern may occur in certain words or letter combinations, or perhaps only at the beginning or end of a word.

Letters toward the end of words or signatures occasionally diminish in size, often due to writing speed. In other cases the writing size may increase at the end of words, although this is less common.

It should be noted that the buckle of the small letter k is commonly enlarged and must therefore be considered less significant to identification unless it is also unique in some way. Similarly, the letter r is often written proportionally larger than other letters in the same script, so that it also should be viewed with care.

While size is more or less habitual, it is to be noted that it may be influenced by the amount of available writing space. When placing a fair amount of written material into a limited space (as on pre-printed forms) the natural tendency is to write smaller. On the contrary, while people are capable of writing larger than normal should they so desire, usually there is not an appreciable increase in the size of one's writing when given a larger than necessary writing space.

Writing size may also be influenced by the degree of speed with which the pen travels across the writing surface. Fast writing tends to re-

1. Klara Roman, Handwriting, New York: Pantheon Books, 1952.

sult in a reduction of size, especially of midzone structures. Careful, deliberate writing is often produced on a larger scale and may entail more vertical strokes compared to swift writing which is generally smaller and leans more rightward.

A deliberate change from small to large or vice-versa (usually the former) may be chosen as a method of disguise. Such an alteration will have some effect on the pictorial appearance of the script, but it is somewhat difficult to maintain for an extended period and the person will usually revert to his or her normal writing habits within a short time.

Pressure

Pressure is the downward force of the writing instrument onto the paper which manifests as thickness, darkness, sharpness or shading of the writing. The degree of pressure may fall anywhere on the spectrum of extremely light to extremely heavy, although in most writings there will be some variation of pressure as the pen travels across the page, giving a lively quality to the script. Seldom is an entire writing produced with unchanging pressure.

There is no practical way to measure the degree of pressure and the examiner must therefore rely on observation of indentations in the paper, distribution of ink, embossing on the back of the page or displacement of the paper's fibers by the pen tip.

Due to the influence of different writing instruments, estimates of pressure cannot be based strictly on the width of writing lines. Some, like felt tip pens, require little or no pressure to create a thick line. Others, such as a fine tip ballpoint, will leave no more than a narrow trail even when considerable pressure is applied.

It is also inadvisable to rely on photocopied material when estimating handwriting pressure. Photocopiers produce density according to the amount of toner they are depositing. A copier set to the highest density or one that is in disrepair may result in a heavy, black reproduction of writing. Conversely, a copier at the lowest density setting or one with a nearly depleted toner supply would result in seemingly light line writing. In addition, writing on multi-generational copies deteriorates and/or takes on added thickness with each successive copy. A true estimate of the writer's pressure patterns can be accomplished only by examining the original document.

Generally, downstrokes (those that are made by drawing the pen toward the writer's body) tend to be executed with more pressure than upstrokes which move away from the body. This occurs due to natural release and contraction of the hand muscles which creates a light up, heavy down pattern. However, this will vary from one writer to another.

In natural, non-deliberate handwriting the writing instrument is already moving when it makes contact with the paper, causing the beginning of the initial stroke to be tapered or feathered. A gradual increase of pressure ensues as the pen moves on to complete the first stroke. When the pen is lifted, the pressure is naturally and gradually decreased, also producing a degree of tapering as it does so.

Non-variable pressure is a factor that comes into play with most poorly imitated signatures or tracings where there is a drawn, labored appearance and a lack of natural movement. In such writings, initial and terminal strokes are apt to be blunt. Consider that some people naturally write with rather constant pressure, so it is important to know if this is usual for the writer by examining adequate comparison standards.

In some cases writing pressure becomes displaced so that upstrokes are written with increasing heaviness. This is sometimes apparent in the upswing of lower zone loops but may also be seen in upward moving initial strokes of upper zone formations. Horizontal strokes may also be written with greater or lesser pressure than the other strokes in the writing.

Circumstances may influence the degree or distribution of pressure in one's writing. With tension or stress there may be a stronger grip on the pen and added pressure. With illness, weakness or injury to the writing hand, the grip may be lessened and the pressure decreased. Elderly people sometimes have difficulty maintaining effective control over the writing instrument and may write with weak and/or variable pressure. Writing position can also affect pressure.

Spacing

The writer's use of space is often a significant factor in determining authenticity. Letter, word and line spacing are to be examined.

One's habitual treatment of spacing is derived from practice, based on the handwriting model, which gradually results in involuntary fixed patterns. These patterns only vary within certain limits. For instance, when a person is forced to write in a small area the overall size of the writing may decrease, but proportions and spacing remain relatively consistent.

Spacing routines do vary from individual to individual as do other characteristics in writing due to conscious or subconscious modifications by the writer. Despite similar training, background and experience, people produce varying degrees of individuality in this regard.

However, the examiner is cautioned that "normal" spacing should not be heavily relied upon for identification or elimination purposes due to its commonality with a large number of people. Extremes and exceptions are always more revealing.

Line spacing

While this subject technically relates to arrangement, it will be considered here with other spacing concerns. The distance between writing lines varies from one individual to another, ranging from very close to far apart. In some writings the distance decreases or increases as the line travels across the page. Some writers crowd their lines to the extent that loops from one line intersect the adjacent line or lines; other writers leave more than adequate room from one line to the next.

Most individuals maintain fairly constant line spacing. However, of note in this regard is that a writer is more apt to decrease the space between lines rather than decrease the relative spacing of words in a line when the writing area is restricted.

Line spacing is simply measured by marking the bottom of the midzone letters (the baseline) of each line and then measuring the distance between. If there is considerable variation of distance from line to line, the average of the distances is to be used. When spacing narrows or widens toward the end of lines, those distances should also be taken into account.

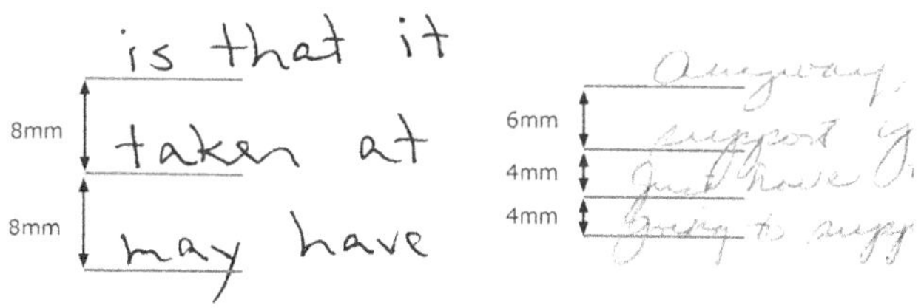

Fig. 4.8—Measurement of line spacing. Line spacing of first sample is 8mm. Average line spacing of second sample is 5.3 mm.

Letter spacing

Distance between letters is dictated by whatever handwriting model the writer studied, but individuality nevertheless develops. The continuum is from exceptionally narrow to extra wide. As with line spacing, distance between letters does not usually vary appreciably within an individual's normal writing.

Wide distances between letters gives the writing an airy or expanded appearance, while closely spaced letters creates a tight impression. When extremes in letter spacing occur, they become more significant than when the person uses moderate spacing.

Letter spacing is effectively measured in letter widths rather than in millimeters or fractions of an inch. The difficulty with precise measurements is that distance between letters may differ at the baseline as opposed to the tops of letters. Overlaying the writing with a transparent grid will offer an instant look at spacing as well as other writing features. (See Figure 4.9.)

Of particular importance are those groups of letters in a given writing that are spaced uniquely. It is common to observe letter pairs like o-u placed close together, while i-n-g is often more spread out. A review of such common words as the, and, from or that will reveal a writer's natural variation when producing those words and will also alert the examiner to any unusual letter spacing habits.

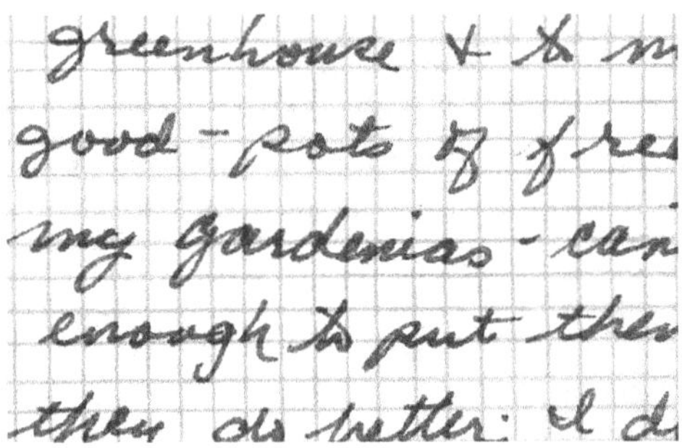

Fig. 4.9—Grid overlay to determine letter spacing

When a handwriting is simulated, the forger will generally pay attention to details of letter design and general spacing but will seldom observe and correctly imitate any unusual groupings that are characteristic of the genuine writing.[2]

2. Wilson Harrison, "Handwriting—Spacing, Slope, Shading and Line Quality,"

Word spacing

Recommended spacing between words varies according to different writing systems. Some dictate that the distance be equal to the width of the lower case letter m or the width of the child's pencil or finger. In all models word spacing is meant to be consistent which gives the writing a look of uniformity.

As with other spacing, distance between words varies from one individual to another. Words may follow closely upon each other or be written far apart. Extremes will be more revealing than modest word spacing which is more common.

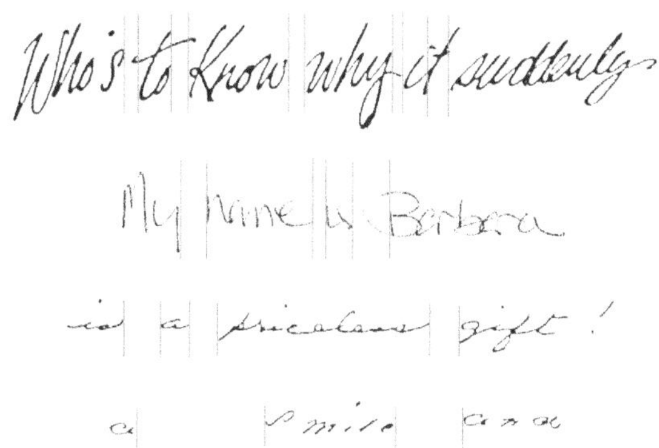

Fig. 4.10—Word spacing measurements

Spacing in signatures is an important consideration. In falsified signatures the spacing between names is often incorrect due to the person focusing on letter formations and also writing at the incorrect speed.

Connecting Strokes

In ancient times there was no need for connecting strokes between individual characters as writing was limited to chiseling inscriptions in stone or clay. The demand for more rapid writing caused Egyptian hieroglyphics to gradually became distorted and more linear. Similarly, squared Roman capitals written on parchment or papyrus, began to assume a more fluid, connected appearance. With the gradual evolution of cursive handwriting, scribes found that writing could be produced more quickly and easily if the pen did not have to be lifted after each letter. As the pen could remain on the paper, various types of individualized strokes eventually developed to link letters together, allowing writing to become truly cursive (derived from the Latin word *currere*, to run).

School children normally learn to form printed letters first, which they later link up in cursive writing. The shape of cursive letters is stressed more than the type of letter connections formed between them, leaving room for individuality in the connectors.

Wilson Harrison wrote that "most writers have fixed habits with respect to the nature and placement of their connecting strokes, which means that these strokes, especially when they diverge widely from copybook forms, are of considerable value for the characterization of handwriting. As this is so, it is fortunate that a wide range of variation will be found for the length, curvature and placement of the connecting strokes in contemporary handwriting."[3]

There are four primary types of connection strokes: garlands, arcades, angles and threads. The connectors used by the writer are often also employed in writing individual letters, particularly *m, n* and *h*, which contributes to the writing's overall form.

Garlands, which represent the simplest and most common connection between letters, are gentle curves written in a counterclockwise direction that resemble the letters *u* and *w*.

Arcades are rounded formations most typical of children's writing, but often carried into adulthood. These formations are opposite to garlands in that they are written in a clockwise direction, such as the arches of the letters *m* and *n* in copybook writing.

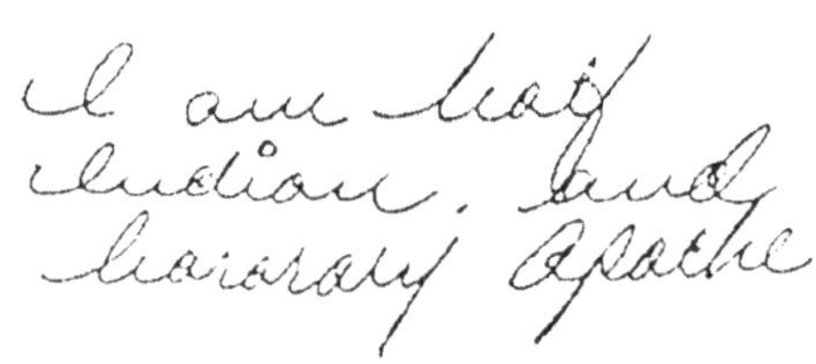

Fig. 4.11—Garland connections

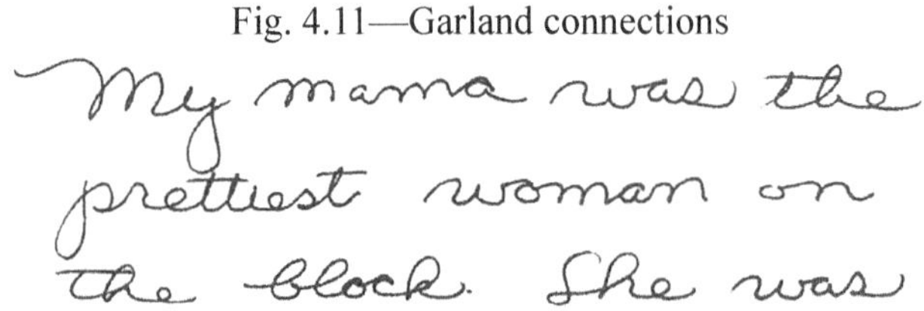

Fig. 4.12—Arcade connections

3. Wilson Harrison, "Handwriting-Connecting Strokes," Journal of the World Association of Document Examiners, Vol. 15.

Angled connectors result from abrupt changes in pen direction. In succession they create a saw-tooth appearance which lends a look of stiffness or rigidity to the script.

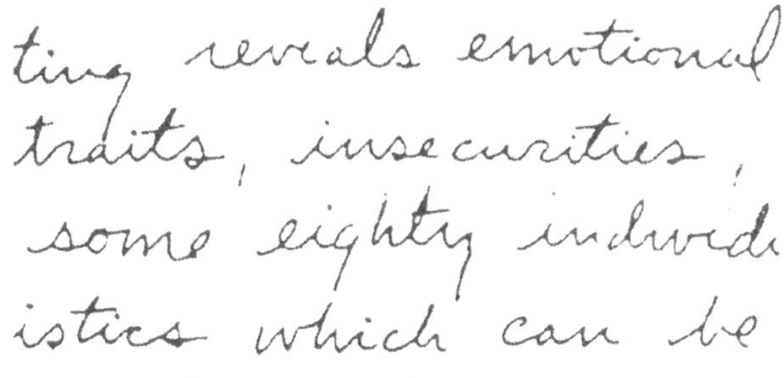

Fig. 4.13—Angular connections

Thread formations lack definition and may cause "slurs" in the writing. Often the result of speed, they sometimes cause writing to appear scrawled, ill formed or indefinite.

Some writers utilize only one of the four types of connectors, but in most cases two or more are used. It is possible that one type of connector will be used for certain letter combinations in a given writing while different letter combinations employ another.

Fig. 4.14—Thread connections

In some instances the connection of particular letters dictates the form utilized. For example, because the lower case e normally terminates at the baseline, the natural movement to the next letter is counterclockwise, calling for a garland movement. On the other hand, the small letter o normally terminates at the top of the letter and can most easily be connected by a clockwise (arcade) movement to the next letter. Any departures from these usual connectors are indicative of individualism.

In addition to the primary form of connectors utilized, the length and degree of curvature or angularity of these strokes may be significantly personalized. Also, any minute divergences (such as an odd bend or glitch in the stroke) should be noted.

In simulated writing, the forger usually fails to recognize the significance of connecting strokes, often using the wrong form or executing them with uncertainty. This is naturally a strong sign pointing toward inauthenticity.

Letter connections are of course not necessary to legibility or even the overall structure of writing. In manuscript (printing or handprinting) each letter usually stands apart from its neighbors, making for fewer connectors than in cursive writing. However, connections are not precluded and, in the case of printscript, there are connectors between some letters and breaks between others. (See section pertaining to printing later in this chapter.)

Hiatuses and Pen Lifts

The dictionary definition for hiatus is a pause or gap in space, time or continuity. Most writing systems allow for no gaps between letters except those that follow capitals. Therefore, the inclusion of hiatuses is largely personal, with some exceptions. When and if a break occurs in a word, it is natural to place the break between syllables. Such breaks may consequently have little identification value. Likewise, breaks after capital letters are rather common and relatively insignificant.

The evidential value of hiatuses depends to a certain degree on the letters on either side of the breaks. Placing a break before letters c, d, g or o is quite common and, as a result, not very telling. This is due to the reluctance of many writers to slow down the writing process in order to fully form the retraces necessary to connect these letters to the letters that occur just before. Many people habitually lift the pen before writing h, m, n and t and after the letter q. Somewhat common, breaks in these places are not strongly evidential.

Breaks placed before the letters i, e and v, which are normally connected to previous letters, are more likely to be individually significant.

Even more compelling than the break itself is its positioning and the distance between the pen lift and the placement of the pen back onto the paper. Sometimes such breaks leave a barely perceptible gap, while others are quite wide. Most writers adhere to a fixed distance when creating such breaks, even when attempting disguise. Breaks between letters have the greatest value when they are observed in one writing but not the other, suggesting uncommon authorship.

Hiatuses within signatures are highly individual and especially revealing. Often forgers inadvertently lift the pen at the wrong place or fail to break between letters where breaks ought to be. When individuals attempt to disguise their own signatures so that they can later deny them, they nearly always include breaks in the proper places of the disguised signature, which helps lead to identification. The spacing of the capital letters of a signature is of great importance, especially with signatures of semi-literates, for this is (according to Harrison) "one of the few features in which such persons exhibit consistent writing habits."[4]

Pen lifts may be distinguished from hiatuses in that a hiatus creates a gap between letters while a pen lift usually occurs within the stroke of a letter. Generally pen lifts are less apparent than hiatuses.

Pen lifts (especially when they are inconspicuous and perhaps only visible microscopically) can be important identifiers. This is particularly true when the names of a genuine signature are written continuously but an alleged simulation contains breaks in the writing line. These are likely to be indicative of the forger literally taking a break to ensure that the simulation is being done "correctly."

It is also possible, however, that a person can be momentarily interrupted while signing their name in which case an accidental pen lift may occur. If extra care is taken to replace the writing instrument at the exact position where it was lifted, there is more evidence for non-genuineness, particularly with regard to signatures of the elderly or ill who may be incapable of such precise repositioning of the pen.

Another type of inadvertent pen lift sometimes occurs in the upstrokes of upper extenders and, less commonly, in upstrokes of lower case letters. In such instances the pen momentarily skims above the page, leaving a feathered edge where the lift occurs and also upon re-entry to the writing line. This is generally the result of the combined effects of writing speed, light writing pressure and slight pen grip. (A "heavy," non-feathered beginning or ending to such a break is not apt to be natural and may be indicative of forgery, although illness and writing position must also be considered.)

Seldom are such skips of the pen observed in downward movements

4. Wilson Harrison, Suspect Documents, Chicago: Nelson-Hall Publishers, 1981.

where more force is usually applied to the writing instrument, the grasp is stronger and the pressure greater, therefore creating less opportunity for the pen to lift. Pen type and condition might have an effect here, so the writing should be examined carefully.

Initial and Terminal Strokes

Initial or lead-in strokes are beginning movements of the pen which lead into the formation of the first letter of a word. Lead-in strokes can be garland, arcade, angular or thready in formation. They can take on any shape or size and are optional in that regard.

They are considered individual characteristics of the writing, yet sometimes vary within the same writing depending on which letter they precede. They may be more pronounced when leading into a capital letter, for example. In many instances they are omitted almost entirely from an individual's handwriting, or they will be dropped only from certain letters. The writer can alter initial formations at will and care must therefore be exercised in evaluating this feature.

When considering the possibility of two different writers, it is important to examine the beginning of initial strokes. If the pen was in motion before touching the paper, the start of the initial stroke will have a tapered, feathered effect. Some document examiners refer to these strokes as "flying starts."

Fig. 4.15—Flying starts, finishes

Terminal or final strokes are those which immediately follow the formation of a letter or word. As with initial strokes, terminals take on different shapes, sizes and directions according to the writer's personal habits. The copybook recommendation is an outwardly directed movement with a slightly upward tail, formed like a cup. However, few writers adhere to the model so that final strokes are written with heavy pressure or light, move upward, forward or downward, end bluntly or with a taper or hook. They may be strong and direct or weak and wavering.

Proportions of final strokes are relatively constant. And as more conscious attention is normally focused on the beginning of letters, words and lines, final strokes are more apt to be individually characteristic than lead-in strokes.

The ends of final strokes must be examined to determine if the pen was still in motion upon leaving the paper, in which case the strokes will be tapered. Blunt finals suggest that the pen stopped momentarily before being lifted from the paper while blunt initial strokes indicate that the pen rested momentarily on the paper before moving forward. Both are signs of deliberateness or simulated writing, although caution is advised as they can also occur in genuine writing. As always, adequate and comparable exemplars are necessary.

Fig. 4.16—Blunt initials and terminals

Embellishments

Embellishments consist of flourishes, ornamentation and underlinings. While simplification reduces unessential parts of letters, embellishment adds unessential strokes.

These added curlicues and flourishes appear at the beginning and completion of capital letters and often at the end of lines. They sometimes adorn signatures or appear as t crosses. They can take on any form, but are often circuitous, spiraled or whiplike. When done in an artistic way they give the writing a look of grace and finish, but they may seem garish and clumsy in less accomplished handwritings.

When simulated, unusual ornamentations are generally produced in an awkward fashion. Embellishments should be viewed for shape, size, location, spacing, direction and movement.

Abbreviations

Abbreviations are shortened forms of words or terminology designed to save time and space. They were utilized extensively by secretaries and scribes of old who took down dictation at court and needed shortcuts in doing so.

Mathematical and scientific abbreviations are common, as are those representing academic diplomas and degrees, titles, military ranks, and political designations, to name but a few.

Abbreviations may be placed into three main categories: suspensions, contractions and arbitrary signs. Suspensions utilize the first letter or letters of words to represent the whole. Common suspensions are A.D. (Anno Domini), A.M. and P.M. (ante- and post meridian) and "etc." (et cetera). Suspensions may also include acronyms that stand for organizations like UN, CIA, FBI and IRS.

Contractions involve the use of the first letter(s) and the last letter(s) of words such as *Wm.* for *William*, *Mr.* for *Mister* and *blvd.* for *boulevard.* Many contractions entail placement of an apostrophe to represent the dropped letters (it's for it is, can't for cannot).

Arbitrary signs are also representative of words or concepts and include symbols like the "at" sign (@) and the ampersand (&) as well as scientific, medical, mathematic and musical designators.

Abbreviations are habitual with regard to design, placement, proportion, size and alignment. They are especially prevalent in informally handwritten material and can be quite diversified from one individual to another. For example, California might be abbreviated as *CA, Ca., Calif.* or *CALIF*, with or without punctuation.

Rules regarding the formation and writing of abbreviations are imprecise, rendering them inconsistent from one writer to another, and at the same time arbitrary. Regarding abbreviations *Webster's Legal Secretaries Handbook* states, "No rules can be set down to cover all possible variations, exceptions and peculiarities. The style of abbreviations—whether punctuated or unpunctuated, capitalized or lower case, closed up or spaced—depends most often on the writer's preferences..."[5]

Envelopes readily display abbreviations such as *Mr., Mrs., St.* and *Ave.* Characteristic ways of writing these abbreviations remain fixed over many years and are rarely altered, even under the influence of disguise. Consequently, their identification value is high.

---

5. Coleen K. Withgott, General Editor, *Webster's Legal Secretaries Handbook,* Springfield, MA: G. & C. Merriam Company Publishers, 1981, p. 196.

*"Forward" refers to direction of the writing. In Latin alphabets the direction is from left to right, but in some cultures writing moves right to left, in which case forward would mean leftward

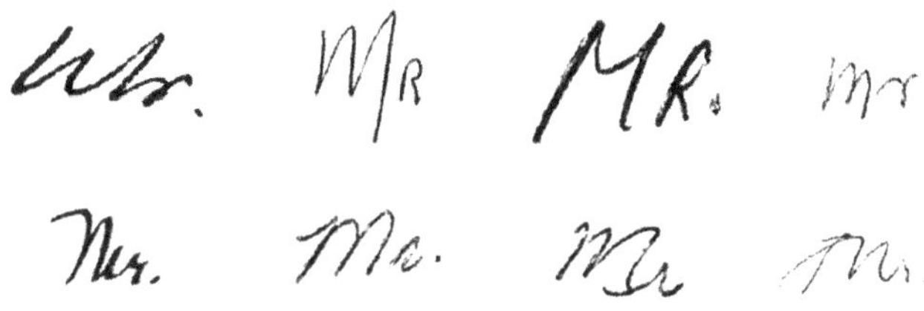

Fig. 4.17—Envelope abbreviations

Slant

Slant is defined as the tilt of the handwriting strokes away from the upright or vertical position with respect to the baseline of the writing. The majority of handwritings have forward slant or slope, varying from almost vertical to far forward. As forward slant* is employed so universally it is apt to have little individual significance, with some exceptions as noted below.

Writing slant is influenced by the positioning of the pen to the paper, the hand to the writing surface, and the angle of the paper to the writer's body. It is possible for a left-hander to achieve a fluid, rightward motion by adjusting body position and paper, so there is little evidence to support the popular notion that left-handers' writing typically slants leftward.

Slant is determined by measuring a representative sample of letters and strokes, preferably in succession. Strokes in all zones of the writing—middle, lower and upper—should be considered. It is up to the individual examiner as to whether to measure slant on the upstrokes of letters or on the downstrokes, as long as the same method is followed consistently. Using the upstroke method, slant lines are drawn as illustrated below and then measured by using a protractor positioned along the baseline. Normally slant is indicated by degrees to the right or left of vertical, e.g. +30° or -30°.

Average slant may be calculated by adding all of the slant line degrees and dividing them by the number of slant lines. However, this exercise is not particularly effective in proving authorship. It is more productive to consider the relative slant of different letters to each other, and the slant patterns that result. During the simulation process, the forger often fails to maintain the same slant rhythm or pattern exhibited in the known signatures. A variable, uncertain slant may result and the relative slant of neighboring letters will consequently be disrupted.

Fig. 4.18—Slant measurements. Genuine (top), simulated (bottom)

Slant should be evaluated carefully because a change of this writing feature alters the appearance of the writing, and slant is usually the first choice for attempts at disguise. It is commonly known that a person's feelings at the time of writing can affect the slant as well as pressure. Slant can also shift more toward vertical when the writer changes from hand and finger writing to just finger writing. A tightly held pen or pencil permits primarily finger movement and usually results in smaller, more vertical writing.

Consistent slant patterns between handwritings may support identity, but different slant may be due to writing position or pen grip rather than a different writer. A slight but persistent difference in the slant of two writings may be evidence that they were produced by two different writers. However, a pronounced difference in slant of 10 degrees or more may indicate disguise.

Punctuation, Dots and Diacritics

Punctuation

The purpose of punctuation marks in handwriting or printed material is to clarify meaning. Punctuation divides writing into sentences and parts of sentences so as to provide pauses and accentuation, and to inform the reader of emphasis or subtleties of meaning. Included here are periods, commas, question marks, exclamation points, colons, semicolons, quotation marks, parentheses, brackets, dashes and apostrophes.

Punctuation probably developed from the need to convey natural breathing pauses in such a way that the meaning and rhythm of language would not be disrupted. Eventually, such signs came to suggest interruptions in thought and gradually became an integral part of sentence structure and meaning.[6]

Punctuation marks are more or less consciously produced and are "part and parcel of the manner in which both writer and reader understand the symbolic representation of spoken language."[7]

Writers' punctuation habits are relatively inconspicuous and therefore useful for identification. A simple period, comma or question mark can be highly significant in some cases. As most writers are unaware of the formation and placement of these characteristics they usually do not change them when attempting disguise. In Harrison's discussion of punctuation and diacritics he notes that "being inconspicuous features, they are rarely disguised as their significance is not appreciated."[8]

The form, position, height and direction of punctuation marks are all important and, in combination, become individually characteristic. Space between punctuation and preceding and following letters is often distinctive. There are writers who habitually elongate, abbreviate, exaggerate or repeat punctuation marks (for example, "*!!!!*" or "*????*")

The degree to which a person utilizes commas may also be important; some use them wherever possible, others less often. Establishing a pattern in this regard can be useful in writing comparison. Absence of punctuation may be encountered and must be considered as potentially evidential as well.

In the past few decades apostrophes—normally used in place of missing letters or numbers or to indicate possession—have been increasingly used improperly, particularly in attempting to make words plural, but instead rendering them possessive (e.g., *cat's* or *dog's* instead of *cats* or *dogs*). The commonality of such errors may render apostrophes less valuable evidentially with respect to misuse, but their formation, direction and placement will be significant.

Other punctuation like exclamation points and question marks can be highly individualistic and the writer may be tempted to use such unique formations even during disguise. Baker states, "Although parentheses may not be exactly the same in curvature and brackets may not be

---

6. Klara Roman, *Encyclopedia of the Written Word*, New York: Frederick Ungar Publishing Co., 1968.

7. Mary I. Duncan & Baryl Gilbertson, "Dots, Dashes and Other Marks in Handwriting." Journal of the World Association of Document Examiners, Vol. 26, p.1.

8. Wilson Harrison, *Suspect Documents*, Chicago: Nelson-Hall Publishers, 1981.

the same in size each time they are written, those of one writer possess a general uniformity which distinguishes them from those of another."[9]

As with numbering and arrangement patterns, punctuation on envelopes can be very important in the identification process, particularly when investigating anonymous writing, because it is seldom disguised.

Dots

Dots and periods can be particularly revealing with respect to their placement relative to the preceding word and the baseline. In the case of signatures, periods will be positioned relative to initials, or not utilized at all. Dots in general are affected by writing speed. The faster the writing, the more likely dots will become dashed, jabbed or connected to the following letter or word. "Flying dots" will indicate pen direction and may be useful clues as to authorship.

Precise dots, on the other hand, require slow, careful placement of the pen point. This indicates slow writing or at least a momentary slowing down of the writing action to produce such a dot. Often these dots will be placed with exactitude after the last words of sentences.

The pressure of periods and dots, which lies anywhere on the continuum of very light to very heavy, may also be revealing. "Dots" can be curved or angular, convex or concave. Sometimes dots are perseverated—written over and over and perhaps even ground into the paper. Circle dots are of course rather common and sometimes hearts or *x*s are used.

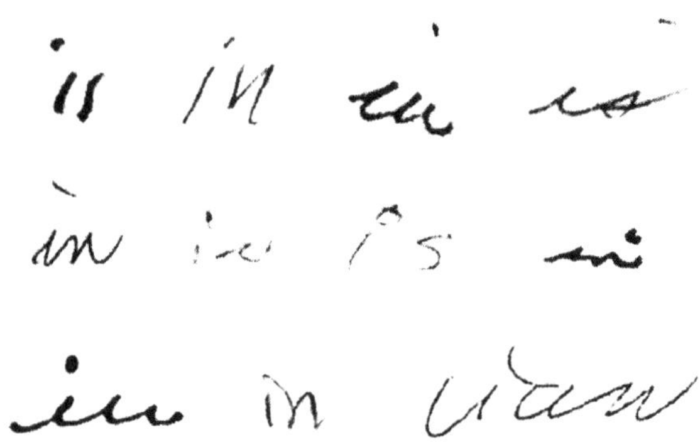

Fig. 4.19—Various *i*-dots

9. J. Newton Baker, *Law of Disputed and Forged Documents*, Charlottesville, VA: Mitchie Co., 1955.

In addition to the overall shape and direction of i dots, the examiner would be wise to consider the placement of the dot with respect to the stem of the letter—before, above or ahead as well as how high.

Dots are so important that their omission may also be significant. In some cases forgers neglect to incorporate dots that are present in the signature they're simulating. In other instances they create the required dots, but do so deliberately so that the resulting mark does not have the movement proper to other features of the signature. Dots in forged writing are often too carefully placed and too slowly executed.

Diacritics

Diacritics are defined as modifying marks or signs placed on letters to distinguish them from similar letters and/or to indicate a phonetic or semantic value. Diacritical marks include, but are not limited to, the accent (both acute and grave), cedilla, circumflex and tilde. English is free of such marks, but there are of course foreign words incorporated into the language which make their use imperative. Most written languages do utilize diacritics and they should be examined with respect to both class characteristics and individuality.

Signs and Symbols

Symbols act as shorthand for many disciplines—scientific, mathematical, medical, electronic, musical, chemical and astrological. Proofreader's marks and religious signs can also be included here. Most written signs originate in some profession or discipline but eventually make their way to the general public. Common symbols are @ (at), # (pound or number), *$* (dollar), *£* (British pound), ¢ (cents), *&* (ampersand), *%* (percent) and * (asterisk).

Symbols are executed a variety of ways and are certainly written with uniqueness and individuality. Edna Robertson states that "symbols are products of habit and often carry greater identification value than some letters in words and names."[10]

Any symbols that appear in an individual's writing should be studied carefully for unique formation, placement, slant, size, proportion and alignment. Dollar signs can be made with one vertical stroke or two. They can be placed in line with the numbers that follow or may

10. Edna W. Robertson, Fundamentals of Document Examination, Chicago: Nelson-Hall Publishers, 1991.

ride higher. They can be written vertically or with a forward slant. The number sign or octothorpe (#) should be examined for slant and for placement of the horizontal strokes relative to the baseline. The length of both the vertical and horizontal strokes of this symbol should be considered, as well as their proximity and degree of parallelism to one another.

Check marks and cross marks, such as those used to tag information or identify choices (as in voting) are also valuable identifiers as they are often quite unique. Check and cross marks may come into question when a person claims they did not mark certain boxes on forms.

With cross marks, the examiner can consider their size as well as the pattern or balance of the two strokes, remembering that they often do not meet perfectly in the middle. Their placement relative to the item they are next to or the box they are in may also be significant. With check marks the examiner will consider the overall size, relative size of the two strokes, slant of the mark, degree of angularity formed by the two strokes, placement with respect to the line or item to which it refers, and degree of curvature of the two strokes, especially the second of the two.

The ampersand (&) can be especially revealing in that it is somewhat difficult for even skilled writers to create fluidly. Like other symbols, its construction is not stressed as much as the formation of alphabet letters in the model, so individual writers have more freedom in its style and execution. It may therefore take on various shapes and sizes. As with other symbols, its overall style, positioning, proportion and proximity to other letters should be reviewed for idiosyncrasies.

Printing

Printing refers to various types of non-cursive, disconnected lettering systems. The use of block capitals, sometimes called lettering, is common to draftsmen, engineers, architects and commercial artists. In its true form, it is relatively rare, although printing consisting of all capital letters ("all caps") is somewhat common.

Manuscript writing, also referred to as lower case printing, is a combination of both upper and lower case letters. It is commonly taught in early grade school before students advance to cursive.

Fig. 4.20—Professional block printing

Another form of printing is printscript, a cross between manuscript and cursive where the material is essentially printed but various letters are joined up with connectors.

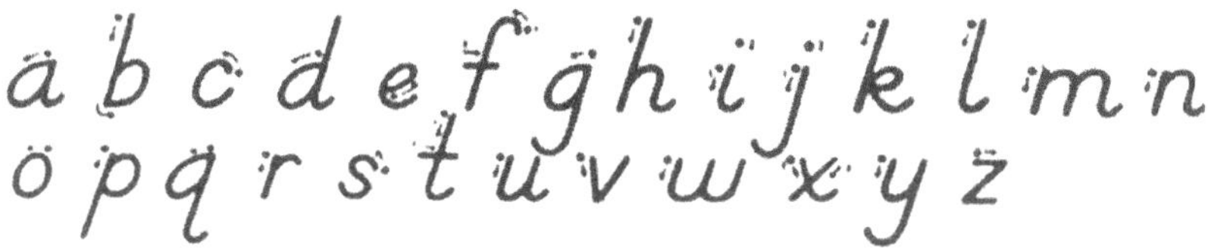

Fig. 4.21—D'Nealian manuscript

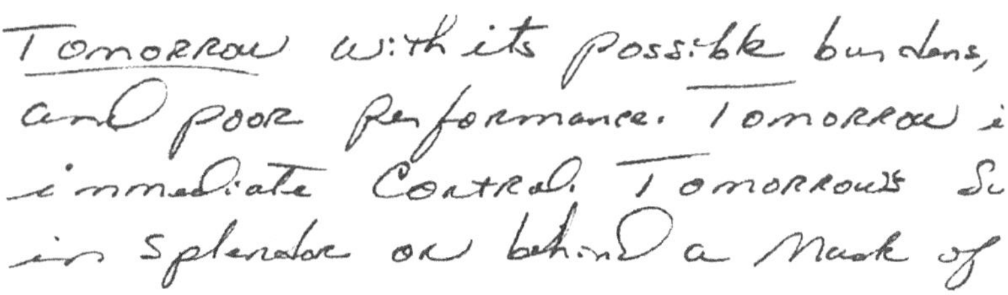
Fig. 4.22—Printscript

Nowadays printing is as prevalent as cursive writing, particularly considering that handwriting in general is given less attention in school children's curricula. Printing is used in most public and private organizations and is required on personnel forms, employment and credit applications, government papers, drivers licenses, bank documentation and a myriad of other forms. Many people choose printing over cursive for at least some of their business and personal communication. Printed signatures are even becoming more common.

School children normally learn printing before script. Cursive writing, which involves sideways connectors, is taught later when students are expected to have developed sufficient motor skill to write smooth lateral movements. Amend and Ruiz suggest that boys often lag behind girls in developing motor skills and they tend to become frustrated at the ineptness with which they produce cursive. Often, they opt then and there to stick with printing.[11]

Some people utilize printing because they believe their handwriting is illegible, while others claim they can print faster than they can write. This is unlikely as every lift and replacement of the pen between printed letters detracts from speed.

Like cursive, the forms and overall structure of printing are based on a model. Consequently, a review of the less obvious features will likely be more revealing than the style of the printing.

It might seem to the layperson that basic printed letter forms are the same between one person and another. In fact, few people use the small letter printing they were taught, but instead develop individual characteristics that become habitual and identifiable. The versatility of the printer is limited only by ability and imagination.

In most respects the comparison of printing is the same as cursive writing and the examiner will therefore consider basically the same features. Some printing consists primarily of downstrokes, resulting in an absence of connections between letters, which have an important impact on writing movement. Consequently, other elements like size, ratios, spacing, punctuation habits, letter design and construction must be evaluated.

When handling an assignment involving printing the examiner should first consider whether the printing in question may have been disguised. Fluency of movement and certainty of execution will point toward a measure of skill and naturalness. If the printing appears to have been created with conscious mental effort and is lacking in fluidity, disguise is a possibility, although further investigation will be necessary before reaching that conclusion.

A side-by-side comparison will quickly determine if the same style of lettering was used in both the questioned and known printing. If not, the comparison probably can go no further as the exemplary standards are of improper form, unless there is some idiosyncrasy that ties the two together. Under most circumstances the basis for the comparison of printing to cursive writing is negligible.

Conway states that "to be identifiable, a handprinting subject to inquiry must contain the individualities and characteristics of its author in

---

11. Karen Amend & Mary Ruiz, *Achieving Compatibility with Handwriting Analysis*, North Hollywood, CA: Newcastle Publishing Co., 1992.

adequate kind and number, and it must receive adequate evaluation in comparison with adequate exemplars of handprinting of the author."[12]

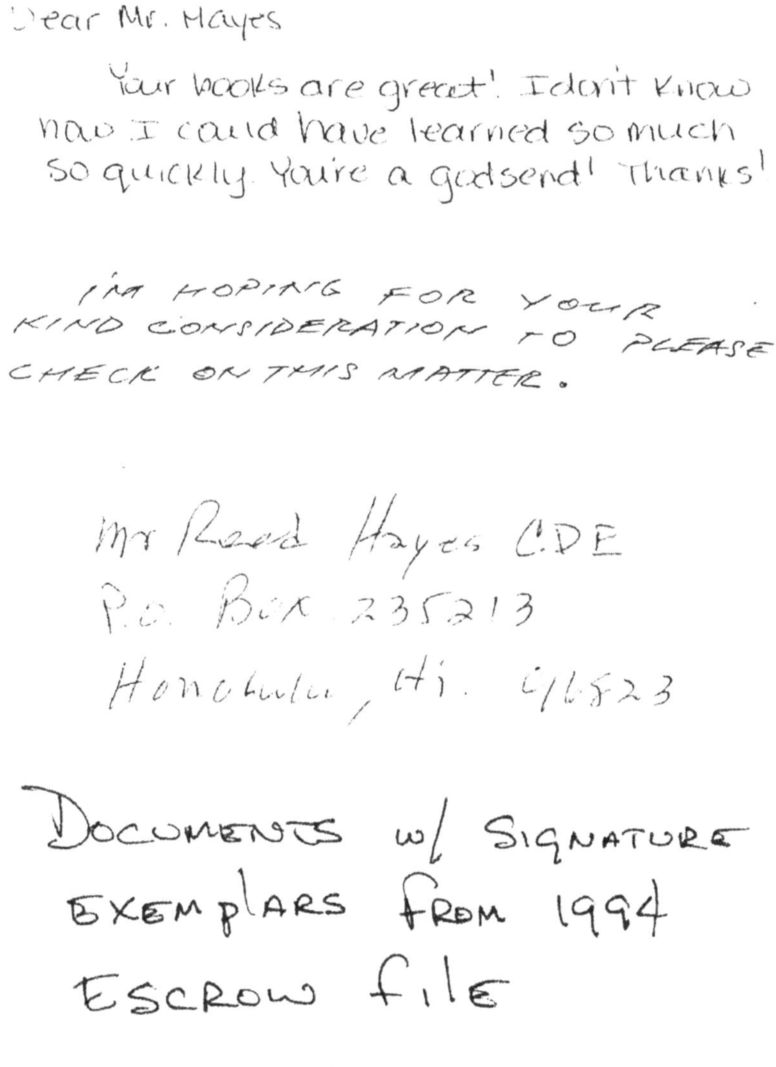

Fig. 4.23—Various printing styles

Some people have the misconception that a mere switch from cursive to printing will be sufficient for attaining disguise. This will hold true only providing there are no adequate and comparable printed exem-

12. James Conway, *Evidential Documents,* Springfield, IL: Charles Thomas Publishers, 1959, p.59.

plars available for comparison.

A common method of disguise is to print with all capital letters. The advantage is that block lettering usually does not give the appearance that it is disguised. Also, while it is generally easy to obtain specimens of cursive handwriting for comparison, block lettering is less apt to be available, unless that is the suspect's usual form of writing. Due to this fact alone the use of all capital lettering as disguise is sometimes effective. But if comparable material is available for examination, identification is possible.

Numerals

Numerals are often significant components of handwriting cases, particularly with respect to financial issues including accounting records, payroll matters, tax concerns, fraudulent checks and suspected embezzlement. Dates are often at issue and the handwriting examiner may be called upon to verify authorship of same.

Forgeries often involve numbers. Manipulation can take the form of erasure, replacement, rearrangement or reconstruction of numbers. Some figures lend themselves to ease of manipulation, such as changing *1* to *4*, *6* or *7*, or turning *3* into *5*. Also common is adding zeros after already placed numbers, obviously to raise the value of the instrument.

There is a somewhat limited number of general shapes prescribed for numerals, yet idiosyncrasies do develop and handwriting examiners agree that figures are in fact individual and identifiable.

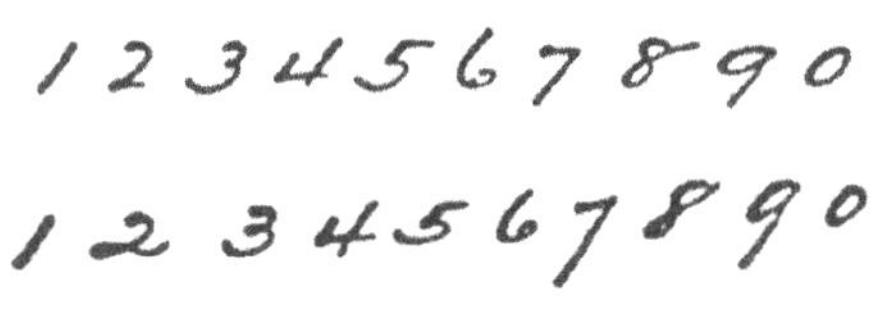

Fig. 4.24—Copybook numerals. Zaner-Bloser (top), Palmer (bottom)

In general, the evaluation of numbers is similar to examining handwriting and handprinting, especially the latter which also consists largely of disconnected characters. Like other features of writing, the numerals 0-9 can be evaluated for individual shape, alignment, relation to other numerals, direction of movement and proportions. The inconspicuous features are likely to be of more help than the shapes of numerals in working toward conclusions regarding authorship.

Quirke suggests that the alignment of numerals should be studied closely as "not twenty percent of writers, even among the best educated commercial classes, align all their numerals according to conventional usage."[13]

Many writers use more than one class of numbers according to the documentation at hand. Different types of numerals may be found on ledger sheets than on envelopes addressed by the same individual, and some classes of numbers may be used interchangeably.[14] Also, people often have a wide range of natural variation when writing numbers. These possibilities are of course important considerations, especially where comparison standards are concerned.

Numbers *8* and *0* vary somewhat between individuals in their starting point or, more specifically, their stroke direction which is dependent upon the starting point. Clockwise *0*s, sometimes written by left-handers, can be significant to the matter at hand.

Although they are sometimes the only thing in question, numerals are more often associated with other handwritten material. They are frequently accompanied by symbols like dollar signs and plus, minus and equal signs which, as previously pointed out, are often unique.

Many times the person attempting disguise overlooks numerals, leaving them basically unaltered in formation. Some go no further than turning the usual fluid *8* into a snowman figure, or adding a cross to the *7*.

Combinations of numerals are more apt to be revealing than those standing alone, particularly given their relationship to one another with respect to size, spacing and alignment. They are sometimes uniquely connected to one another which can lend important clues, as will any unusual punctuation or placement, such as when writing dollar amounts on checks. The manner of writing cents units on checks should be considered as well as characteristics like percentages, placement relative to the line or box provided, whether or not there are underscores and, if so, how they are written.

Not every number related case can be conclusively resolved. Cases involving a limited amount of numerals are particularly difficult and, as

---

13. Arthur J. Quirke, *Forged, Anonymous and Suspect Documents,* London: George Routledge & Sons, Ltd., 1930.

14. Lee A. Kilty, "Numbers," Journal of the National Association of Document Examiners, Vol. 11, No. 3, August 1990, p.14.

in all questioned handwriting cases, sufficient standards are necessary.

Spelling

There is no question that certain words in the English language are difficult to spell, and that some people have trouble spelling even simple words that others spell easily. Spelling mistakes can be the result of mispronunciation or the writer's personal misapprehension as to how they should be written.

Generally, uneducated writers are less likely to closely follow spelling and grammar rules than those who are better schooled. When an educated person makes spelling errors, either 1) the mistakes are due to intentional disguise, in which case they will usually not appear in both the questioned and known writing, or 2) the errors are inadvertent and the writer consistently makes them in good faith.

However, there are other considerations and possibilities, so the examiner should exercise common sense. Odd spelling may be the result of dyslexia which can also cause reversals of letters (*b* for *d*) or improper letter sequencing (*was* for *saw*). Some misspelling is deliberate, especially in disguised writing, while some is unintentional and goes unnoticed by the writer.

To the layperson, misspelled words in documentation are apt to be conspicuous and might be considered proof of non-genuineness. To the handwriting examiner, they will likely not be given so much weight. Words like *ninety* and *forty* are often spelled incorrectly and such words as *their* and *there* are commonly confused. Consequently, they may not be very strong evidence for authorship.

Harrison rightfully suggests that caution be employed in considering spelling errors else they end up playing too great a role in legal proceedings. He writes that when rather simple words are repeatedly misspelled they are apt to be significant, unlike more difficult words that are easily misspelled by many people. Writing environment for environment would be less telling than using hear instead of here, as the former example is the likely result of a common mispronunciation whereas the latter is probably more personally characteristic.

If, in considering a questioned writing, a rather difficult word is spelled correctly on at least one occasion, then it becomes obvious that the writer knows the proper spelling. Proof of a suspect's ability to spell would depend on evidence in the comparison standards provided.

Saudek noted that peculiar spelling habits, along with variations of different forms for the same character, are more significant in comparisons than the actual shape of individual letters. He also suggested that unusual spelling habits, syntax and grammar may help lead authorities to the writer of anonymous letters.[15]

Obviously, for habitual misspellings to prove valuable as key identifiers of the author of anonymous writings, they must also occur in comparison standards. However, the examiner must consider that in some cases writers make deliberate errors in grammar and in the spelling of simple words normally spelled correctly even by poorly educated people. When exceptionally easy words are misspelled, indications are that the writer may be trying to create an impression that an uneducated person is the author.

Ordinarily a person will not misspell his or her name unless rushed, in which case one or more letters may be omitted or slurred. Misspelled names do sometimes appear in fraudulent signatures due to slip-ups of the forger, but this is not always conclusive evidence for non-genuineness and must be corroborated by other findings.

Sometimes misspellings occur in signatures on genuine documents like wills which are disputed primarily for that reason. A signer can easily make such a mistake due to accident or by hurrying. Illness, influence of medication or alcohol, or interference during the signing process can also cause such disparities. In such cases letters are usually omitted, but rarely added. It is possible for an elderly, ill and/or medicated person to misspell words or names, which warrants inquiries regarding the circumstances at the time of signing.

Comparison material written by a suspect after the production of a questioned writing may not be very helpful in this regard as the person then has the opportunity to deliberately misspell the words that are properly spelled in the questioned writing, or vice-versa.

Spelling is sometimes at issue with respect to request exemplars, as in the famous Lindbergh baby kidnapping case. The accused, Richard Bruno Hauptmann, complied with police requests—or demands, as the case may have been—for numerous handwritten exemplars. In the exemplars he consistently misspelled certain words which helped tie him to ransom notes. However, there continues to be some question as to

15. Robert Saudek, *Anonymous Letters*, London: Methuen & Company, Ltd., 1933.

whether the material was dictated or if he was shown the improperly spelled text to copy. (An excellent account of the Hauptmann matter is *The Hand of Hauptmann* by J. Vreeland Haring, Hamer Publishing Co., Plainfield, NJ., 1937.)

In *U.S. v. Campbell*, 732 F.2d. 1017 (1st Cir. 1984), a court of appeals ruling reversed a previous conviction where a defendant under court order refused to provide exemplars because he was not allowed to see what he was to write. The court determined the only purpose for the government's insistence on dictating the material rather than showing it to the defendant was to discover his choice of spelling in certain words. According to the court, spelling choices constitute testimonial evidence and a court order forcing the defendant to write would violate his Fifth Amendment privilege against self-incrimination. Testimonial evidence is protected by the Fifth Amendment and its invocation cannot be used against a defendant.

Letter Form/Design

To a certain extent, the formation of individual letters is determined by the model from which the person learned to write. The class or style characteristics of two individuals' writing may therefore be similar and the less conspicuous features must be carefully evaluated to avoid an incorrect opinion of common authorship.

Mistakenly, the layperson often believes that letter forms are the primary writing elements that personalize handwriting. It is not uncommon for clients to present handwritings for comparison, claiming that one writing matches another because the capital letters are similar, the *d*s are formed the same, or the gs are alike. The examiner will of course look to numerous other writing features, alert to the possible presence of class characteristics or the limited number of ways that some letters can be shaped. In fact, letter forms are relatively low on the identification value scale.

Certain letters in a writer's script may have commonalities in overall construction. For example, the circle letters (*a* and *o*) will likely have similarities due to their base formation. Other letters that are partially made of circles (*b, d, g, p, q*) may also resemble the *a* and *o* in their circular component. Likewise, upper loops of the same writing may be similar to each other in formation, size or shading. Similarly, lower zone extensions in the same writing may share common features. It is up to the examiner to determine the degree of such similarities in a known writing and consider whether the same commonalities exist in the questioned material.

Despite learning handwriting from a model, each person develops his or her master writing pattern according to personal choice and skill, so that specific letters often become individualized. With experience the handwriting examiner comes to learn which letter shapes are truly unique and which are commonplace.

To reach an accurate assessment in any handwriting comparison the examiner must consider the influence of natural variation. How often does the known writing exhibit a particular letter form, and how much does that form vary within the writing sample? No writer will execute a letter identically from one time to the next. Some writers exhibit a wide range of variation regarding specific letters, while others are more consistent. Also, the same letter in an initial, medial or terminal position in a word may be written differently.

As indicated by Harrison, despite any variation, a writer's master pattern for individual letters will usually remain unaffected whether the writing was produced carefully or carelessly, the writer was fatigued or rested, or a different writing instrument was used.[16]

The writer's usual habits with respect to individual letters must be established before an accurate comparison can be made. It is suggested that each capital and lower case letter be considered in order to assess their overall construction and variability within a given writing. If each letter of the alphabet is taken in turn, there is less chance for overlooking anything pertinent. Looking beyond basic letter forms, the examiner must be alert to any idiosyncrasies in specific letters which will of course make them more valuable for identification purposes.

It is a rather common mistake for beginning handwriting examiners to point to similarities or differences in isolated letters, rather than reviewing them in groupings with other letters that surround them. Individualism often shows in the relation of one letter to another and therefore the arrangement, spacing, ratio and alignment often become more significant than individual letters, unless of course they are very personalized on their own.

The examiner's task can be facilitated by comparing entire words

16. Harrison, *ibid.*, p. 303.

between the questioned and known writings. Common words such *as the, and, at, from* and *or* can be quick indicators of authorship.

Capital letters are perhaps the least reliable structures for identification purposes. They often follow the form prescribed by the writing model, which may make them common to a larger group. They are one of the more obvious features of the writing and are therefore more likely to be altered in disguise attempts. Additionally, the forger seldom overlooks these obvious letters.

Pen Direction

In some questioned writing cases, pen or stroke direction may be a significant consideration. Different line direction can be indicative of different writers. For example, one writer might habitually make clockwise circles in forming a "snowman 8" while a forger attempting to simulate that person's number 8 might write the circles in a counter-clockwise direction.

Characteristics of ballpoint pen writing are often revealing where direction of movement is concerned. The examiner should consider the presence of three possible characteristics: cold pen starts, striations and ink globs. Any or all of these may be observed in ballpoint writing, although in some cases none will be evident.

Cold pen starts are evidenced by a deficiency of ink flow at the very beginning of writing movements caused by the pen literally not being warmed up prior to the writing. Ballpoint ink is more viscous at lower temperatures and sometimes does not flow properly onto the ball portion of the pen until friction and pressure increase its temperature and fluidity. This explains why it is sometimes necessary to scribble with a pen until it begins to work properly.

The result is a lack of ink deposited onto the paper for the first portion of the writing line, as illustrated in Figure 4.25. The presence of this phenomenon helps to confirm the beginning of a writing stroke or a passage of writing. Cold pen starts are sometimes seen at the beginning of signatures where the writer may or may not touch up the missing ink.

Striations are also typical of ballpoint pen writing and are very useful in determining stroke direction, particularly with respect to curved formations. Also known as burr striations, they are evidenced as scratches or streaks within the confines of the ink line's edges. They are caused by obstructions such as lint, paper fibers or debris that collects on the ball and prevents the proper flow of ink. Sometimes striations are visible to the naked eye and in other cases they can be seen only under high magnification.

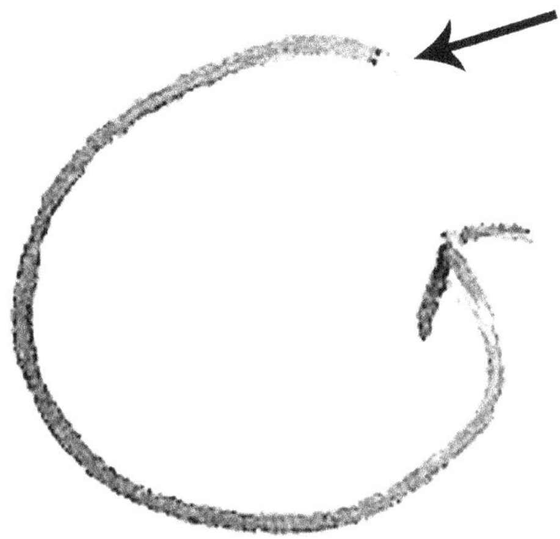

Fig. 4.25—Cold pen start

Striations run longitudinally within straight sections of the ink line and enter or exit the ink line in semi-circular formations. When they appear in the curved portion of a stroke, they always move in an outward direction with respect to the curve, exiting on the outside of the curve. This makes it relatively easy to determine direction of movement.

Ink globs or gooping are also useful in the consideration of stroke direction. Globs of ink often collect on the pen's ball housing and deposit onto the writing surface following movement around curves. This typically occurs at the bottom of lower loops and the top of upper loops where the pen changes direction. They may also deposit along connecting strokes and sometimes in small letters. Such deposits can be seen inside the writing line or on its outer edges.

Pen direction can be determined as the gooping occurs after the pen has moved around a curve. (See Figure 6.5.)

To reiterate, each of the handwriting features discussed in this chapter must be evaluated individually and collectively prior to reaching conclusions as to authorship.

Fig. 4.26—Ballpoint pen striations. a=clockwise movement; b=counter-clockwise movement

5. Complex Writing Features

Movement

Obviously, without movement there would be no handwriting. Writing movement is a function of the fingers, hands and arms and is accomplished by the interrelation of the brain, the muscles and the nerves which all integrate on a subconscious, habitual level. The movement of one's writing reflects the predominant actions of the writing tool and dictates the shapes and forms recorded on paper.

Writing movement is largely automatic. It determines the pictorial quality and overall form of the written product. With continued practice, form becomes more or less automatic as well, but it is still dependent upon the writer's movement patterns. Habitual movement is more difficult to deliberately change than is the form of writing.

Writing movement is directly dependent upon one's eye-hand coordination and is closely tied to skill level. It is also affected by other factors such as the writer's neuromuscular condition, visual acuity and depth perception.

Finger, hand and forearm movement

In slow writing with deliberate movement, only the fingers are involved. This is referred to as finger movement and is the first method used as children are learning to write. It requires frequent shifts of the hand which interferes with the rhythm and flow of the writing so that poor line quality is characteristic.

Some writers naturally utilize essentially finger movement. But slow, calculated writing can also be indicative of the forger who is focusing on the right production of letter shapes rather than the flow of the writing.

Finger movement can often be identified by halting movements, inconsistent width and direction of connecting strokes and some uncertainty in the writing trail. There is usually little freedom in the writing stroke, and a general lack of lateral expansion. With finger writing there tends to be more emphasis on the midzone of the writing so that upper and lower extenders are often proportionally short.

Free arm (or forearm) writing is produced by movement of the full arm from the shoulder. This utilizes the primary muscles of the arm with the wrist and fingers playing a secondary role. Such movement allows maximum speed and produces a continuous writing trail characterized by smooth line quality. To accomplish free arm writing requires practice, in addition to a certain amount of natural skill.

Fig. 5.1—Finger movement

Forearm writing normally consists of smooth, sweeping movements of the pen. Lee points out that with forearm movement the writing displays "speed, force, freedom, continuity of motion, uniformity of pressure, and usually a uniform baseline."[1] Most significantly, the line quality will be smooth and consistent and the writing will be rhythmic.

Fig. 5.2—Forearm movement

Most people are more skilled than finger writers but less adept than forearm writers. They use a combination of wrist and hand movement which results in greater freedom of expression than finger movement, faster and better rhythm, and a tendency toward more rounded forms. However, wrist and hand movement lacks the sweeping quality of forearm writing.

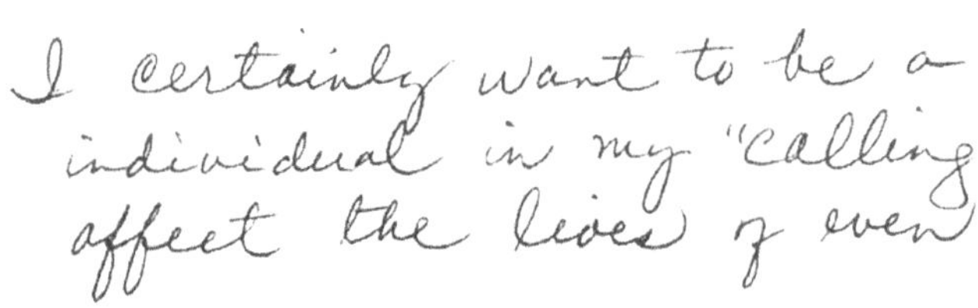

Fig. 5.3—Wrist/hand movement

1. C. D. Lee, Classification and Identification of Handwriting, New York: D. Appleton & Co., 1922.

Writing Skill

An individual's writing skill is largely dependent upon movement. It reflects one's ability or proficiency in the writing process which develops over time with practice and repetition. Children first learning to write are of course unskilled so that individual letters are often clumsy and disjointed. Eventually, as letter shapes become more familiar and hand and eye coordination develop, letters are linked together and the child's writing usually begins to take on more rhythm and fluidity.

Writing skill can be thought of as being on a continuum, with the unskilled or deliberate writer focusing on each aspect of the writing, and the highly skilled and practiced writer performing the task more or less automatically. The primary resulting difference is the slow, deliberate writing of poor line quality of the unskilled writer who uses mostly fingers and thumb versus spontaneous writing normally characterized by smooth line quality as written by the more skilled writer who utilizes muscles of the entire arm.

Good writing skill results in smoothly executed lines and formations that are normally written with speed and without interruption. Due to relatively little focus on how the writing is being produced, there is freedom of movement and a natural flow to the writing.

With skilled writers, movement generally starts before the pen actually touches the writing surface and finishes as the pen leaves the writing surface. This results in tapered starts and finishes. Line quality is good, upper and lower zone formations are often proportionally large in comparison to midzone letters, and loops are usually full and extensive.

The lower the degree of writing skill, the more deliberate, slow and halting is the written product. Handwriting that is naturally irregular in slant, size or ratio, or that appears clumsy or drawn is evidence of a low skill level.

Writing that evidences gross tremor, which can only be written slowly, is also indicative of poor writing skill and is frequently seen in the scripts of semi-literates. However, simulation or disguise may cause similar tremor as more thoroughly discussed in Chapter 6.

Because writers posses various skill levels, it stands to reason that some handwriting is easier to forge than others. Generally, the writing of a person with poorly developed writing skill, who does not write very often or whose skill has deteriorated, is easier to copy than that of a more skilled writer. Enlarged, swiftly executed curves and loops that require the interaction of more muscle groups are more challenging to the forger than are smaller, more slowly written angles produced with fewer muscles.

A principle universally accepted by handwriting experts is that no one can write better than his or her very best. This concept implies that under ideal conditions a writer will perform optimally. One who has diminished or undeveloped writing skills cannot be expected to produce handwriting demonstrating superior letter formations, connections and rhythm. Therefore, suspects with normally inferior writing can be instantly eliminated when the authorship of skilled writing is under investigation.

Likewise, it is somewhat difficult (although not impossible) for a more skilled writer to successfully imitate writing of inferior skill. In doing so the person may unconsciously reveal their true writing abilities in occasionally fluid movements, smooth curves and nicely rounded circular formations.

Rhythm

Rhythm is the flow of writing movement as marked by the interplay of variation and repetition in tempo, timing, spacing and stress.[1] It is that indefinable "something" about a writing, more readily perceived than quantified, which gives life and dynamism to the script.

The assessment of rhythm in handwriting is rather subjective because it cannot be practically measured. It arises from the physiological and perceptual-spatial-motor makeup of the writer[2] and is closely related to timing. It is difficult to describe or demonstrate to the layperson, but is very significant to the handwriting examiner.

Most authors on the subject relate rhythm to regularity and form level, the aesthetic quality of the writing as judged from the overall appearance of the script. They generally focus on "good rhythm" evidenced by contraction and release of the writing hand which creates a light up, heavy down pressure pattern.

Ordway Hilton called rhythm "that element of the writing movement

1. Klara Roman, Encyclopedia of the Written Word, New York: Frederick Ungar Publishing Co., 1968.
2. Beryl Gilbertson, "Rhythm in Handwriting," Journal of the National Association of Document Examiners, Vol. 22, No. 2, June 1999.

marked by regular or periodic recurrences."[3] Harrison noted that its three essential components are regularity in slope, size and curvature. He also indicated that it makes handwriting "pleasing."[4]

Actually, rhythm falls on a continuum and can be loosely evaluated as good, moderate or poor. It is essentially individualistic but sometimes varies depending on circumstances such as what is being written. The rhythm of one word or series of words in a given writing may be more consistent than other words.

Optimal rhythm is produced when a person is writing comfortably and in a normal situation. Rhythm is sometimes adversely influenced by circumstances such as stress, fatigue, illness, interruption of thought, second language difficulties or motor problems like arthritis or writer's cramp. Also, when a writer makes a conscious change in even one writing feature, the overall rhythm is apt to be disrupted.

The degree of rhythm affects the consistency, balance and regularity of one's writing. Truly rhythmic writing is natural and fluent. It moves along in an uninterrupted fashion and is evidenced by good line quality. Positive rhythm results from smooth movement and is a mark of writing maturity. It gives writing an appearance of consistency with similar but not identical movements. It lends balance and fluency without a break in the flow of writing. It is best achieved by forearm movement and is not likely to result from finger movement.

With good rhythm there is apt to be consistency with regard to like elements of the writing. Upper zone formations of the same kind will tend to reach the same height and return to the same baseline level; midzone letters will evidence similar timing in their width and spacing; lower zone extensions of similar type will descend to the same approximate level and return to the same level at the baseline.

Primary factors having a negative effect on rhythm are variation in the slant or size of letters and unnatural breaks between letters. Poor rhythm is awkward, misdirected and of suboptimal line quality. It tends toward angularity which results from unbalanced impulses, and may be hesitant or halting in its movement.

With diminished rhythm a handwriting cannot be produced fluently. Good rhythm comes from reflex action which normally occurs when the

---

3. Ordway Hilton, *Scientific Examination of Questioned Documents*, New York: Elsevier North Holland, Inc., 1982.

4. Wilson Harrison, Suspect Documents, Chicago: Nelson-Hall Publishers, 1981.

writer is thinking about what is being written rather than how. Because disguised or simulated writing is rarely rhythmic, it is highly unlikely that a smoothly executed handwriting or signature with good line quality has been either forged or disguised.

As a very subtle and complex feature of writing, rhythm is exceptionally difficult to imitate. It is nearly impossible for the forger to successfully capture its nuance, so that simulated writing consequently often has a drawn, static appearance.

If two different patterns of rhythm are apparent when comparing questioned writing with known specimens, and if there is no indication that the less rhythmic of the two was written under adverse conditions, there is evidence that the questioned material was not written by the writer of the known.

As suggested by Gilbertson, the speed of a writing may be fast, slow or somewhere between, but it is the constancy of the speed which affects the degree of rhythm, as well as the constancy of the distance covered by each of the writing spaces and elements.[5]

Speed

Not everyone writes at the same pace and therefore the speed of writing may be a significant identifying element, with some limitations.

The velocity with which a person writes is largely dependent on skill level and movement. The script of a proficient writer normally moves along at a rapid pace, while the unskilled writer proceeds slowly and perhaps laboriously. Like other motor functions, speed of the writing hand increases with practice.

The most rapidly written stroke is a straight line, the most direct route between two points. Alphabet letters having the longest lines are generally made with the most speed, while those having shortest lines are written most slowly. Small or narrow letters require more time to write than do larger, broader ones. Perfectly placed, rounded dots are more time consuming than jabbed dots placed well in advance of their intended position. In fact, a correctly formed dot must be made at a full stop.

Anytime there is a change of pen direction, as in writing angular formations, speed diminishes. Consequently, the greater the speed of writing, the greater the difficulty of forming definite angles between two

5. Gilbertson, ibid.

successive strokes.

If a person wants to increase their walking pace, more steps are taken per minute and the length of stride is increased. In like fashion, the faster a person writes, the greater will be the degree of expansion of the writing. Also, any increase in speed will cause a proportionate increase in the slant of the writing.

The speed of one's writing can be varied arbitrarily, but not without leaving traces of the person having done so. Artificially induced slowness is betrayed in a less certain, harmonious line that is sometimes tremulous. Less uniformity in letter size may also result.[6] When a writer tries to deviate from his or her usual writing size, the normal speed of writing decreases.

Determining writing speed

The smoother and less interrupted the writing line, the more rapidly it was created. Straight, non-interrupted lines reflect firm, quick movements. On the other hand, controlled, deliberate writing produces a wavering line lacking in smoothness. Saudek points out that when a person is writing rapidly it is impossible to produce tremulous strokes which are always written slowly and with frequent minute changes of pen direction.

Writing speed can be generally estimated by examining these writing features:

- *Overall appearance*—spontaneity and naturalness versus clumsy, drawn or elaborate.
- *Line quality*—smooth, firm, non-interrupted versus tremulous, uncertain, hesitant, jagged.
- *Directional trend*—forward slant and direction, dots jabbed and/or to right, rightward ending strokes, clockwise circles, extended *t* crosses versus vertical or leftward direction, dots rounded and carefully placed, counterclockwise circles, short *t* crosses.
- *Connective forms*—garland or thready writing, connected formations versus arcades or angles, disconnected formations.
- *Letter shapes*—streamlined, slurred or distorted; tapered initials and terminals; long, slim loops; abbreviated forms or illegibility; neglect of detail versus exact letter formations; blunt initials and termi-

6. Arthur J. Quirke, *Forged, Anonymous and Suspect Documents*, London: George Routledge and Sons, 1930, p.21.

nals; short loops; good legibility; strong attention to detail.

• *Pressure*—medium or light with obvious alternation of thick and thin strokes, clear ovals versus heavy and/or non-varied pressure, blotched or ink-filled ovals.

• *Alignment*—ascending lines, left margin increasing in width versus steadily horizontal or descending lines.

Saudek provided the following basic criteria for deducing writing speed.[7]

Primary Signs of Writing Speed	
Primary Plus Signs (Speed)	Primary Minus Signs (Slowness)
1. Smooth, unbroken strokes; rounded forms.	1. Wavering forms, broken strokes.
2. Frequent signs of rightward movements alternating with leftward tendency at ends of lines.	2. Frequent signs of leftward movement.
3. Great uncertainty of aim after temporary interruptions of the act of writing (after syllable- or word-impulses.)	3. Conspicuous certainty of aim with hardly perceptible deviations from the intended direction of motion.
4. Increased continuity of execution (connection of diacritical signs with the following letter, joining together of words, joining together of numerals).	4. Frequent pauses during execution (meaningless blobs, blobs due to readjustment, angles, divided letters, arrhythmic separations within words, touched up letters.

Saudek also noted secondary signs which increase or diminish the significance of the primary signs. Secondary signs of speed include increasing obliquity as compared with the normal angle of copybook, rising lines with paper and pen positioned at normal angles, and infrequent changes of slant. Saudek's secondary signs of slowness include parallel downstrokes as in copybook, sinking lines and frequent changes of slant.

Pen scope/writing impulse

Pen scope or writing impulse relates closely to the speed of writing. Pen scope is defined as the amount of writing performed before the writer makes a notable readjustment in movement or pen grip, or without a break in the progressive motor sequence.[8]

7. Robert Saudek, *Experiments With Handwriting*, New York: William Morrow and Company, 1929.

8. Jacqueline Joseph, "The Unidentifiable Handwriting: An Anonymous Note Case,"

Some writers' pen scope is limited to individual letters, while others can create several words or entire sentences without an appreciable adjustment in the writing movement.

Letter impulse writing means that readjustments or breaks in continuity occur between each letter. Such a writer produces each word one letter at a time with the writing hand moving to a new position to form each letter. This correlates with finger movement.

Word impulse is when the writer is able to complete an entire word without lifting the writing instrument or making an adjustment in position of the writing hand. Word impulse writing is generally accomplished by wrist and hand movement.

Sentence impulse writing is produced when entire sentences are written without readjustments or breaks. More skill is involved here and the writing is usually created with primarily forearm movement.

Pen scope can be considered a uniquely identifying characteristic, but only if it is repeated in the comparison standards. Consider, however, that writers whose skill limits them to letter impulse writing will not be able to successfully recreate word or sentence impulse writing as produced by the skilled writer. On the other hand, a graphically mature writer could easily downgrade to letter impulse writing.

Journal of the National Association of Document Examiners, Vol. 20, No. 1, Spring 1997.

6. Line Quality

Line quality is an especially significant feature in the handwriting examination process. Along with other identifying characteristics, it is one of the primary elements to be evaluated in determining whether or not a signature is the product of simulation, or if a passage of writing has been disguised.

The term line quality describes the physical attributes of a written line or stroke. Line quality reflects the degree of fluency of the movement involved in handwriting or signatures.

The writing line may be characterized as smooth, fluid and consistent or irregular, halting and inconsistent. It might be heavy, light, firm or uncertain. It might involve tremor. It will display writing instrument anomalies such as a leaky pen. Line quality may be influenced by the writing surface and, in some cases, the media upon which it is written.

The writing line is also referred to as the ductus which Klara Roman defines as "the course of the stroke…the visual record of the path of motion traced by pen or pencil on the writing surface."[1]

Handwriting is an acquired skill that involves the workings of the individual's brain, nerves and muscles. While this interrelationship is more or less fixed and results in habitual writing movements, it is also subject to internal and external influences such as health, age and medications, any of which can influence the quality of the written line.

Good line quality entails smoothness of movement, evenness of pressure or a particular rhythm exhibited by the pressure patterns. The ductus will be free of tremor, jerkiness, sudden changes in pressure and broken or faded strokes. With good line quality curves are smoothly written and there is relatively little, if any, abrupt change in movement, except where it is called for in the design of the letter.

Although the width of the ink line may vary due to pen grip and positioning, in writing of good line quality such variations are smooth and continuous; the actual line will rarely exhibit any sort of distortion. Similarly, a stroke may start as a thin line which gradually widens and deepens, or it may begin heavy and thin out toward the end, but this is gradual and continuous, with no abrupt change in width or depth of impression.

1. Klara Roman, *Encyclopedia of the Written Word,* New York: Frederick Ungar Publishing Co., 1968.

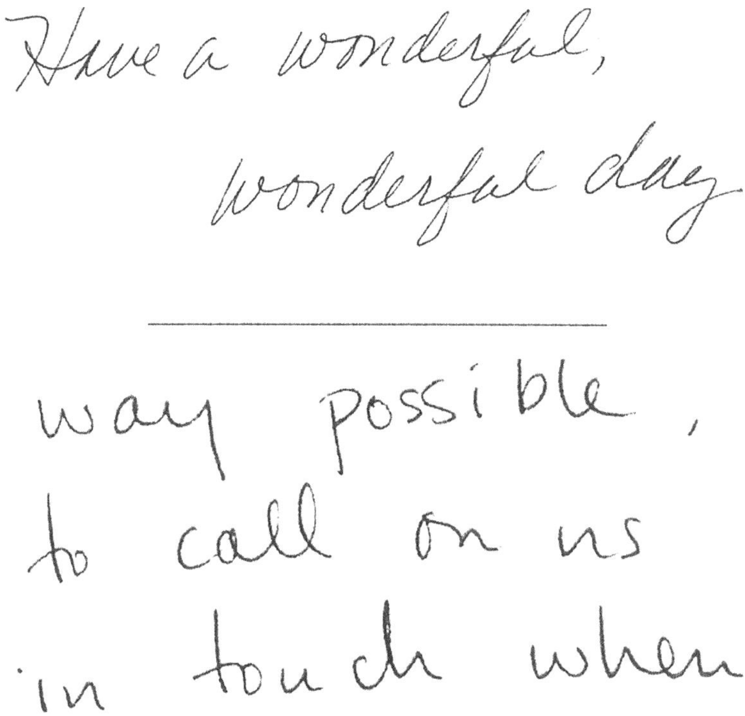

Fig. 6.1—Handwritings with good line quality

To produce handwriting of good line quality, the pen must be controlled by what are largely reflex movements of the hand and arm muscles. Such a handwriting is usually produced when the writer is considering what is being written rather than how.

Poor line quality results when attention is focused on individual movements and letter shapes. This happens with the unpracticed or unskilled writer, or the person attempting to trace or simulate another's writing. In these instances the pen is largely controlled by the fingers which results in writing strokes that lack smoothness and continuity in speed, pen pressure and direction of movement. The writing will lack fluency, the line will be irregular and, in some cases, will take on a labored or drawn appearance.

Handwriting characterized by irregularity, haphazard changes in curvature and lack of smooth transition from stroke to stroke is said to exhibit poor line quality.

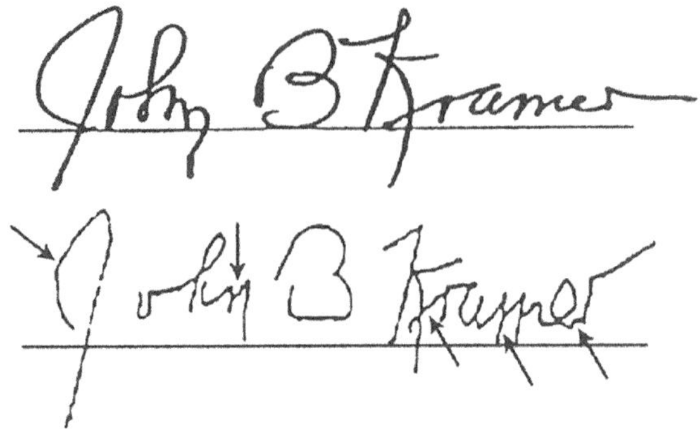

Fig. 6.2—Poor line quality due to simulation

In addition to being caused by the act of forgery or lack of skill, poor line quality may also result from illness, fatigue, poor muscular control, tension, health issues, alcohol or drugs. Writing with the unaccustomed hand will most likely result in poor line quality. Deliberate disguise may be accomplished by utilizing a deliberately distorted line. Immature or underdeveloped writing skills may also cause naturally disrupted line quality.

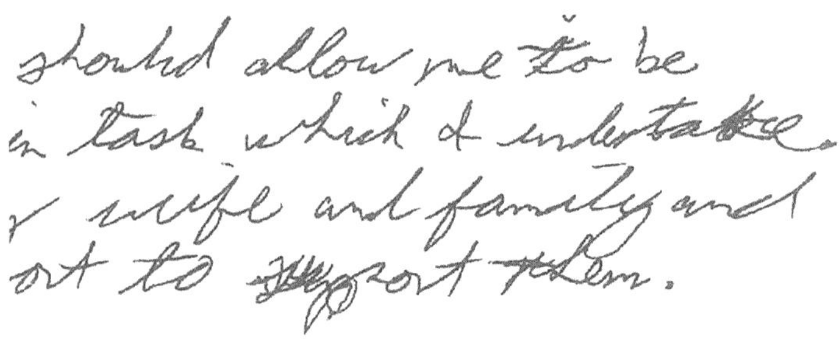

Fig. 6.3—Poor line quality due to anxiety

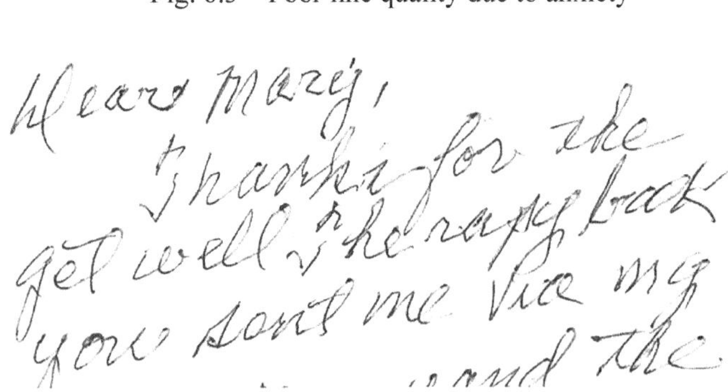

Fig. 6.4—Poor line quality due to illness (heart bypass surgery)

Evaluating Line Quality

In evaluating the quality of the writing line, the examiner should consider:

1. Pen pressure (degree of indentation, ink density and/or line width); whether it is consistent, inconsistent or follows a definite pattern.

2. Flying starts or finishes (tapering of the line caused by the movement of pen as it comes in contact with, or leaves the writing surface); conversely, look for blunt initial and terminal strokes.

3. Degree of smoothness (resulting from smooth acceleration and decelerations of the writing instrument over the writing surface); conversely, the degree of tremor, sudden or unexpected movements or "rough" strokes.

It is these three combined features that are evaluated in determining whether one sample of writing was performed with greater or lesser skill than another, which would help lead the examiner to a conclusion of common or different authorship.

An opinion of different authorship is supported (but not proven) if the questioned writing displays poor line quality as shown by tremor, lack of fluency and/or pressure differentials not evident in the known writing.

Conversely, if the genuine handwriting displays poor line quality and the questioned writing has line quality indicative of a skilled writer, the specimen writer likely did not produce the questioned material. (However, when relying on request exemplars, consider the possible effects of nervousness or attempts at disguise.)

The following terms will assist the examiner in evaluating and describing line quality:

- "Natural," spontaneous, fluid, quick tempo, clean
- Smooth, free-flowing, clearly executed, non-interrupted, smooth stroke edges, consistent pressure patterns, rhythmic
- Heavy pressure/strokes, thick, firm, strong, certain
- Light pressure/strokes, thin, weak, uncertain
- Tremulous, shaky, spotty, disconnected, segmented, frequent pen stops or adjustments, corrugated (unsmooth) edges, jagged, pen rests, variable pressure patterns, arrhythmic
- "Unnatural," deliberate, drawn, slow tempo, pasty

Influence of Writing Instrument

Writing instruments can have obvious effects on the writing trail and the overall appearance of the writing. A pen with a fine flexible point will produce a clear outline, marked shading* and fine details of letter design, no matter how small the scale of the writing (depending of course on the writer's skill level). On the other hand, a blunt pencil will defeat the efforts of the most skilled writer to include either shading or fine detail in the construction of letters. Due to the nature of pencil writing and the usual strong grasp on the pencil, it is least likely to leave traces of distortion in the writing line.

Unlike fountain pens with flexible nibs, the ballpoint pen cannot create appreciably shaded writing. The width of the line is practically unaffected by the pressure being applied, especially when writing on a hard surface, although the depth will be affected and will be more visible if the writing was done on a soft surface. Also, should the ballpoint ink cartridge begin to run dry, the line may be uneven or broken in spite of the point having been kept on the paper. Further, the ballpoint often adds curious circular thickenings to the line when swept around narrow curves. Ink globs or gooping is caused by the accumulation of ink collecting on the ball housing which is then deposited along the lines of writing.

Fig. 6.5—Gooping caused by defective ballpoint pen

As the brain that controls the writing hand remains the same despite the choice of writing instrument, it is only the general appearance of the handwriting and the amount of detail present which are affected by instrument choice. The fundamental structure of one's handwriting remains no matter which writing tool is employed.

* Shading is defined as the contrast between thick and thin strokes that results from alternating degrees of pressure due to natural tension and release of the writing muscles. Upstrokes are usually thinner than downstrokes.

Influence of Writing Surface and Paper

Writing on a very rough surface will likely cause writing to take on a jagged, rough look. The degree of disturbance to the writing line will depend mostly on the writing surface itself as well as on the writing instrument, to a certain extent. The effects of an irregular writing surface or writing on rough paper may appear as repeated or regular patterns of interruptions in the writing line. This is distinguishable from true tremor which does not follow a repetitious pattern.

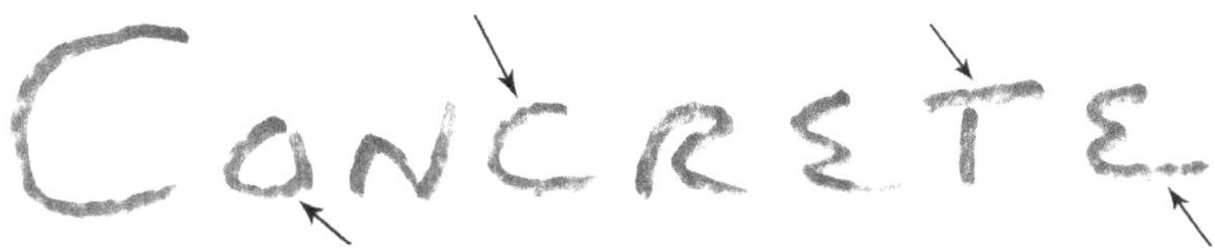

Fig. 6.6—Writing on rough surface. Note uniform pattern of disruption.

Line Quality in Photocopied Handwriting

It goes without saying that original material is always more desirable for the examination process, but handwriting examiners can and do reach accurate conclusions based on photocopied material. However, some considerations are in order.

In 1998 a research project was designed by Dawson and Lindblom to determine which features of line quality are detectable in photocopied signatures. Qualified document examiners from various countries participated in the study in which they were asked to assess photocopies for the presence of tremor, hesitation, pen lifts, patching, blunt initial or terminal strokes and abrupt changes in direction. The study confirmed that characteristics of line quality can be identified in even average quality photocopies. Furthermore, accurate assessments can be made regarding similarities and differences in line quality when comparing a photocopied signature with original known standards. In a few instances, evaluation of photocopies was problematic when striation patterns and ink gooping were misinterpreted as pen lifts, hesitation and patching.[1]

Caution should be employed when examining machine copies, particularly if it is evident that the material is suboptimal. Exceptional care should be used when reviewing faxed handwriting for line quality, as

1. Greg A. Dawson and Brian S. Lindblom, "An Evaluation of Line Quality in Photocopied Signatures" (abstract), International Journal of Forensic Document Examination, Vol. 2, No. 3, 1996.

well as computerized or printed images scanned at low resolution. It is easy to misinterpret the jagged edges of faxed letters as being of poor line quality, when the original may not exhibit poor quality at all.

Tremor

Tremulous writing strokes involve instant changes from the desired direction of the pen line. They are attributed to nervous impulses affecting the muscles involved in the writing process and are of essentially two types: fine tremor and gross tremor.

Fine tremor is generally related to one's health or physical condition. Sometimes called essential tremor, it is caused by some neuromuscular condition and is involuntary. Gross tremor (also known as muscular tremor) results from excessive control of the muscles used in writing, as in the case of unskilled, simulated or disguised writing.

Research has shown that fine tremor occurs at a rate of above six hertz while gross tremor occurs at less than four hertz. They are usually distinguishable from one another in that fine tremor is visibly more shaky or even zigzagged whereas muscular tremor is of a longer wave length and more gradually deviant in its course.

It is not uncommon for some people to have the "shakes"—tremors of the hands or head—which can be temporary or permanent. Shakiness is accepted as part of the aging process and of course has an adverse effect on the fine motor control which is often evident in elderly persons' writing. Such tremor affects an estimated four million people.

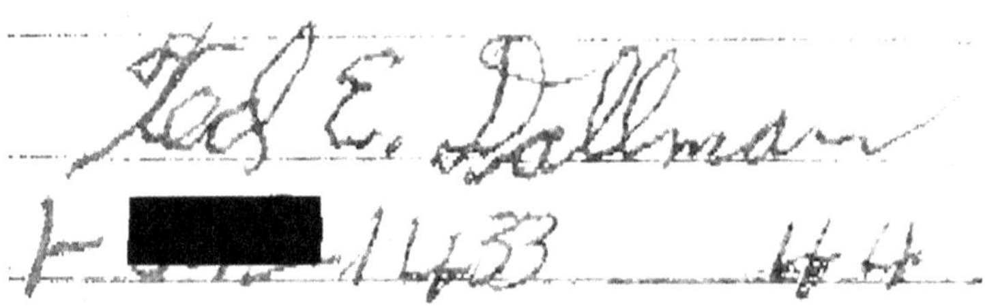

Fig. 6.7—Tremor caused by advanced age

Most often affecting the hands, but at other times the head or the voice, essential tremor (ET) gradually worsens over time. Tremors may occur when the individual is using his or her hands for writing, eating or maintaining a certain position such as holding an object with the arm extended. Fatigue and heightened emotion tend to aggravate these symptoms. ET increases with advancing age, but is fairly common in all age groups and is roughly equal in men and women.

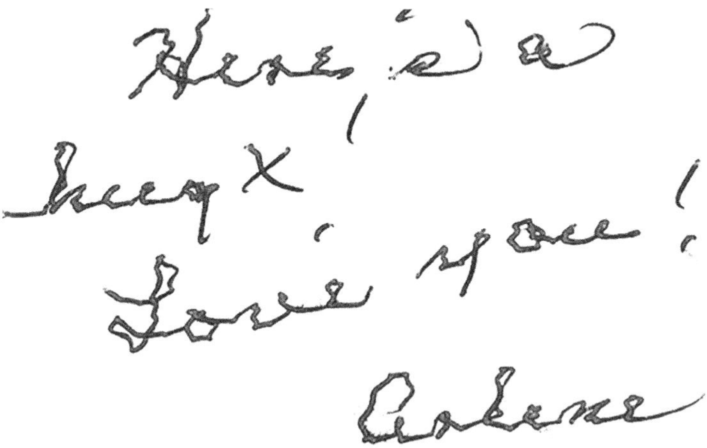

Fig. 6.8—Tremor due to illness

The handwriting of persons with advanced essential tremor is typically large and tremulous, in contrast to the micrographia of Parkinsonism. Essential tremor characteristically disappears during rest, and studies show that writing tremor may be relieved with the administration of a mild sedative.

The course of essential tremor is quite variable and is usually slowly progressive. Tremor beginning in one part of the body may spread to another, and the amplitude of tremor gradually increases. It is not uncommon for a patient to experience tremor for a number of years before finally seeking medical attention.

Slow writing and/or difficulty gripping the writing instrument can also produce tremor in the strokes of writing. Elderly people who cannot adequately grasp or manipulate the writing instrument will necessarily write with tremor.

Tremor is less evident when an individual writes with pencil which is normally held with a tighter grip to render the pressure necessary for the pencil to mark the paper. The tighter grasp of the pencil and contact with the paper help steady the hand and reduce the amount of tremor.

Tremor is apt to increase when the writer's hand has no support (for then the writing is mostly a finger operation), a rough writing surface under the document, or a physical decline causing poor muscular control.

When age or illness affect the handwriting it becomes less coordinated and diminished in skill, legibility and design. More important here, smoothness of execution decreases so that the written line is produced with less certainty. With illness such a decline can occur rapidly, but with aging it will likely be gradual. When a person recovers from illness, the writing slowly resumes its former level of skill, as opposed to aging in which deterioration can only be reversed in small degrees for short periods of time.

Tremor may also be associated with the handwriting of alcoholics who tend to write in a better organized, less tremulous fashion after a few drinks than when fully sober.

Simulation of tremor

As noted, involuntary tremors with fine or weak connecting strokes are often seen in the writing of people whose writing ability has declined due to loss of physical strength. These fine line connections are difficult to imitate. The forger must be aware of their minute features and must possess the dexterity to duplicate them accurately.

Genuine fine tremor consists of involuntary and inconsistent horizontal and vertical lines that are often abrupt and zigzagging. Faking such tremor is often poorly accomplished by deliberately twisting and turning the writing instrument. Sometimes the forger utilizes too much shakiness, or places it in the wrong strokes. When signatures bearing real versus fake tremor are carefully examined, such differences become obvious.

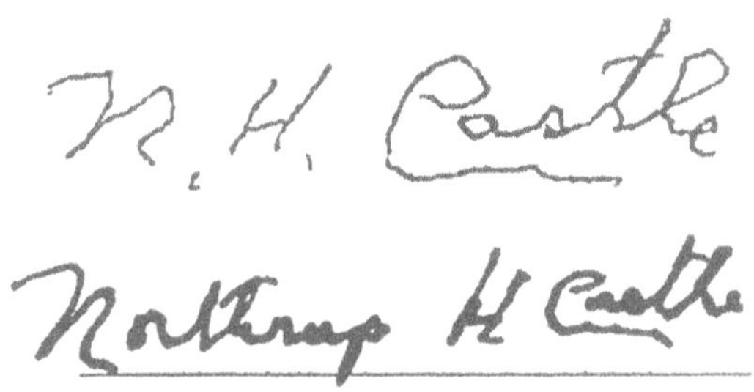

Fig. 6.9—Genuine tremor (top) versus attempt to simulate (bottom). Note in the simulated signature the overly regular "tremor" in the tail of *C* and numerous smoothly written strokes.

Although writing shows tremor in the ductus, there usually remains an inherent element peculiar to the writer that identifies the signature as genuine. Differences between authentic and forged tremor are often more subtle than this, in which case they may be difficult to analyze, and even more difficult to demonstrate to the layman, judge or jury.

Fraudulent tremor

Some causes of fraudulent tremor are:

- The forgery process itself; tremor may not be present in the model writing.
- Imitation of tremor while forging a tremulous model.
- Guided handwriting against the will of the writer.
- Inequality in movement at any place as evidenced by strong line quality combined with weak, hesitating line quality.
- Frequent interruptions in movement, changes in speed or pen pressure.

7. Handwriting Variables

People do not make any movements, including handwriting, with exact precision. This, added to the fact that the writing process, already complicated in and of itself, is influenced so heavily by a number of internal and external factors, writing and the act that produces it are variable. There are natural variations normal to everyone's writing, and changes in handwriting can be caused by age, drugs, medications, illness or unusual writing circumstances.

In the handwriting examination process, the examiner must consider any variables or modifications in the writing under scrutiny in order to distinguish between natural variation and influence by either intrinsical or extrinsical factors.

Natural Variation

Natural variations are normal changes that occur in a person's writing. Such variables are attributable primarily to the fact that handwriting is never produced in a mechanical, precise way.

Normal variation is suggestive of the natural mutability which occurs in every person's writing to one degree or another. Generally variations are superficial and apparent, but in some cases they are more extensive and less noticeable. Some occur frequently while others are only occasional.

Because letter construction is based on the master pattern indelibly impressed in one's brain, primary letter shapes within a given script will usually remain quite similar. But there will always be slight variations in individual characteristics that make up letters or words. Some degree of variation within a writing or signature is a sign of natural movement and genuineness.

Normal variation often entails slight changes in letter shapes, initial and terminal strokes, slant, utilization of space, connections, size, proportions and other features. However, these are minor differences that do not reflect fundamental changes in the writing's overall structure. In other words, even though there are variations, the writing will still be recognizable as coming from one person only.

Natural variation in writing is illustrated in the following chart which consists of the word *the* written five times by nine different writers. Each of the writers produced slightly different letters and word construction while maintaining the same basic master shapes. Variations can be observed in initial and/or terminal strokes, slant, placement and pressure of t crosses and letter spacing, alignment and length. It is readily apparent that each individual set was written by one person, despite the presence of the minor differences. Each set is also easily distinguishable from the others.

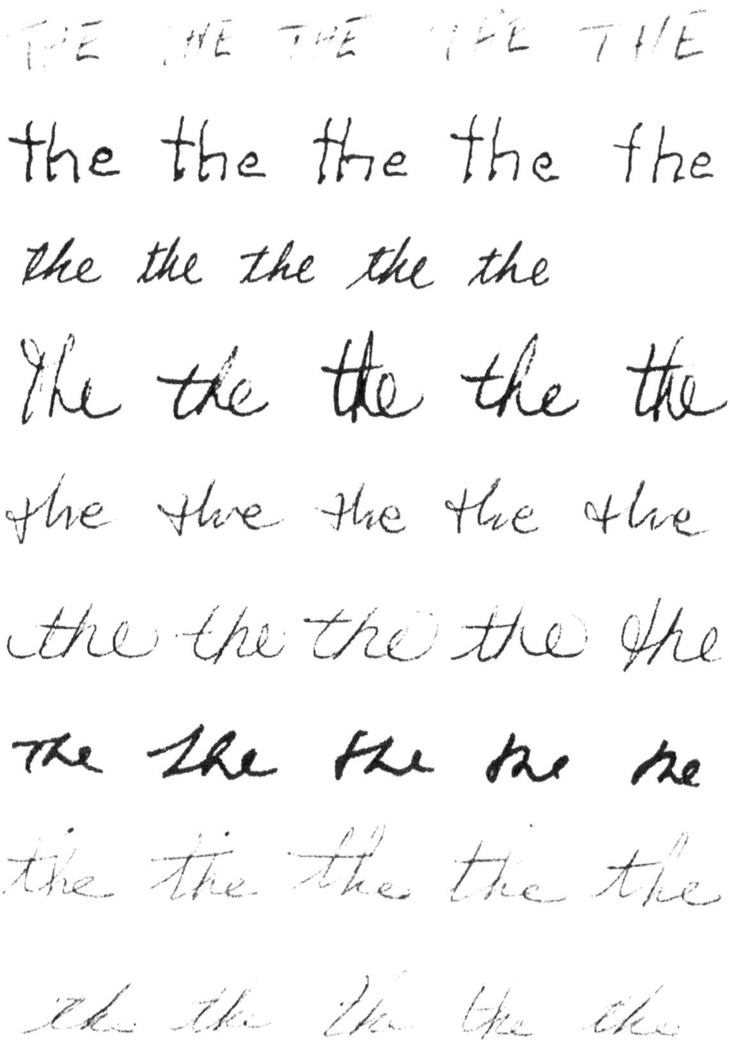

Fig. 7.1—Natural variation of nine writers.
Note variations within each set, as well as differences between sets.

Writers often vary letter forms depending on their grouping with other letters or positioning within a word. The examiner must consider how the shape of a letter changes when it is at the beginning, middle or end of a word.

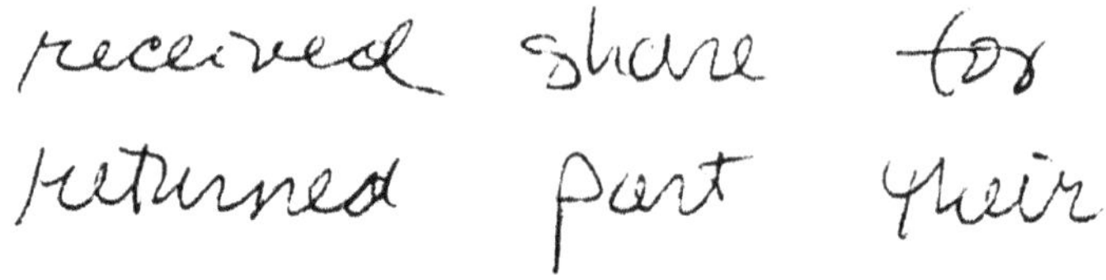

Fig. 7.2—Variation of shape due to letter positioning.
Note different *r* formation in initial, medial and terminal placement.

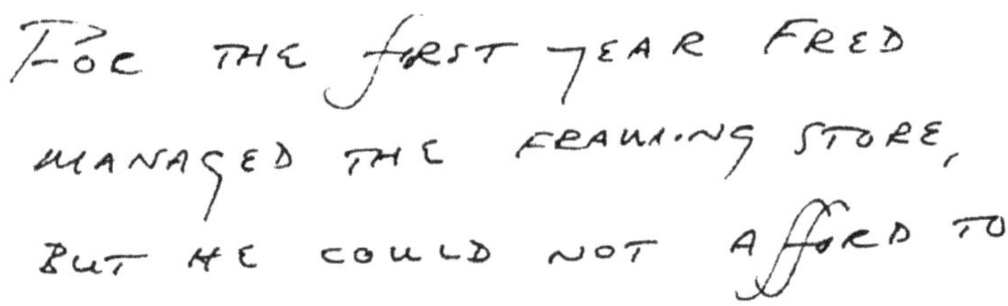

Fig. 7.3—Natural variation in letter form.
Note various capital and lower case *f* styles.

Variation may involve the inclusion of different individual letter forms. For example, some people use variant forms of the same capital letters, depending on the situation. Sometimes they alternate between one letter form and another within the same writing session, as in Figure 7.3.

Identifying natural variation can be challenging for the following reasons:

1. Handwriting variables are different for different writers.

2. The natural range of variation is wide for some writers, narrow for others.

3. Writers can have more than one writing style, requiring numerous comparison standards.

4. Writers have more than one master pattern for each letter shape: at least one cursive form for each capital, a cursive form for the same small letter, a printed form for the same capital letter and a printed form for the same small letter.

5. Letter forms by the same writer will vary according to the place-

ment of the letter within words and their grouping with other letters.

It is more difficult to identify the handwriting of an exceptionally versatile writer. The novice examiner may inadvertently attribute disparities between two handwritings to different writers, when in fact they were written by one person who is simply an inconsistent writer.

The remedy to this possible mistake is to ensure that one has obtained sufficient exemplars written under different circumstances and for different purposes which will be carefully scrutinized for variables.

A study conducted by Lynne Variano, designed for the purpose of determining if there are natural writing habits that are more reliable than others in signature identification, indicated that three areas (shading, letter size and narrow range of variation) ranked highest in overall consistency. Additionally, the height of the l structures were consistently higher than, lower than or the same height as the capitals in the signature.[1]

The examiner should consider that handwriting or signatures of some individuals vary more than others and that numerous comparison standards may be necessary to realize that. Uniform, consistent writing will generally be less variable than more spontaneous writing and the examination will therefore require less in the way of comparison material, perhaps 10-20 samples. With widely variable writing 20-30 samples may be necessary.

The more spontaneous or rapidly executed an individual's writing, the wider the range of normal variation is likely to be, and the greater the number of standards needed to 1) accurately identify the range of variation and 2) distinguish basic differences from that which is normal. For an effective comparison, standards should be adequate in number, cover a specified period of time and be written for a variety of purposes.

Some people utilize two or more very different signatures, such as one for formal documents, another for personal correspondence and another for daily business purposes. It is possible that, presented with the incorrect style of signature for comparison, the examiner may conclude two variant signatures were produced by different people. This highlights the need for sufficient and truly comparable standards.

Given the potential for a wide range of variation or different writing conditions and circumstances, it is more difficult to eliminate than

1. Lynne Variano, "Natural Variations in Signatures: A Pilot Study Endeavoring to Determine Which Writing Habits Are More Consistent," Journal of the World Association of Document Examiners, Vol. 85, p.15.

identify a writer. Ideally, if the circumstances surrounding the suspect writing are known, the exemplary material will be written for the same reason and under similar circumstances which will facilitate the elimination of suspects.

If two or more signatures are identical, there is evidence for non-genuineness. Although writing features are largely habitual, it is impossible to duplicate one's writing movements exactly from one time to the next. Writing can be deliberately changed, but no one is capable of reproducing two identical writings or signatures. To repeat, a certain amount of variation between signatures is a mark of genuineness.

Assessing Natural Variation

An accurate, effective way to determine the degree and type of writing variation is to examine each individual letter of every sample to see how many ways that letter is written. To keep letter forms clearly in mind, each can be copied or drawn onto a worksheet such as those provided in Chapter 9, starting with *A* and working through *Z*. (Using a scanner is an excellent although time-consuming way to copy specific letters and paste them into computerized comparison worksheets.)

The examination must not be limited to letter forms. Other writing features such as word spacing, letter heights, letter and word proportions and alignment (often more valuable for identification or elimination than letter shapes) should be considered in a similar way.

Once this has been accomplished, the same procedure may be applied to the questioned writing. Do the individual letters and other features in the questioned writing fit into the variables established for the known? If the same features are found in both, they were likely authored by the same person. If there are significant differences that cannot otherwise be explained, the conclusion is one of different writers.

Assuming that two people have utilized the same basic alphabet, there will be some similar letter shapes in both writings. If in fact they were written by different people, however, the writings will exhibit letter forms that are consistently different between the two.

The examiner may choose to quickly narrow down the investigation by comparing common words between the questioned and known. As illustrated previously, the word the is often revealing. Even the letter t alone may be instantly evidential as it often varies considerably between writers. Differences may include:

- its basic form
- its height compared to lower case letters, other upper loops and capitals
- looped stem versus retraced
- location of cross bar
- weight, length and direction of cross bar
- beginning and end of cross bar

Disparities between writings that are outside the range of normal variation must be reasonably accounted for as resulting from internal causes, external causes, accident or fundamental differences. There are no hard and fast rules for making such evaluations, although some pointers will be given here.

Accidentals

Accidentals are unusual one-time features in handwriting caused by physical or mental interference. They are rare occurrences that do not repeat themselves. An example of an accidental is when a writer changes his mind during the formation of a letter and then suddenly alters the letter form. Or a writer may be distracted so that a letter becomes misshapen, a word omitted, or extra letters or words added. (Where the writer notices such a mistake, he or she may choose to correct it.) Other accidentals would be sneezing or coughing during the writing process or writing over a crumb under the paper.

Accidentals can occur in any writing, including genuine signatures. Letters in signatures can be repeated or omitted and names misspelled, especially with elderly people. Careful evaluation of such features is important in order to distinguish them from patching or overwriting, sometimes seen in forgeries.

Internal Influences

A number of physical stress factors may significantly alter an individual's writing. Age, injuries or deformities to the writing hand and arm, diseases and afflictions of the central nervous system, problems with the muscles and joints of the writing hand, drugs and alcohol all take their toll on the writing in varying ways and degrees. Emotional response and mental attitude may also affect one's writing.

Intricacies of the writing process require the interaction of many portions of the brain, so that alteration in brain structure or functioning will be reflected in changes in the writing, including size, letter shapes, speed and stability of the writing line.

It is of course impossible to explore here the many effects that these and other circumstances might have on handwriting, although some general observations can be made here. (Alcoholism and the handwriting of the elderly are covered more specifically in Chapter 13.)

Neurological and mental dysfunctions and their relationship to writing have been presented by numerous handwriting experts and researchers. It is well known, for example, that Parkinsonism results in micrographia (small writing which often diminishes even further during the writing process), writing slowness and instability of the writing line. Huntington's disease causes slow writing and macrographia (enlarged writing). Left hemisphere lesions produce dysgraphia (inability to write). Focal lesions in the lenticular formation of the brain or tumors in the basal ganglia-thalmic region can result in micrographia.[2]

Arthritis, a common ailment which entails degeneration of the muscles and joints accompanied by pain, stiffening and swelling, can negatively affect one's psychomotor functioning including the writing process. Inflammations related to this disease are usually intermittent episodes which vary with individuals and age. Debilitating episodes last only a few hours for some, but often days or weeks for others.

When arthritis related pain and stiffness affect the hands, it can make writing a tedious, laborious effort and will tend to produce a writing trail that is diminished in quality. As reported by Miller,[3] a high percentage of arthritic writing involves shaky, irregular rhythm and poor line quality; larger, wider, inconsistent strokes and spacing; frequent pen lifts; heavier than usual pressure; open, broad circle letters often made up of separate strokes; frequent patching; and wider, squared or wedge-shaped loops.

2. E. Edward Peeples & Hans-Leo Teulings, "The Brain and Handwriting," Seventh Biennial Conference of the International Graphonomics Society, London, Ontario, August 6-10, 1995.

3. Larry S. Miller, "Questioned Document Examination of Arthritic Impaired Handwriting," Journal of the World Association of Document Examiners, Vol. 108, p.4.

Unlike the diminutive writing of Parkinsonism patients, the handwriting of psychotics is characterized by large, swift and freely written movements. However, as Marcel Matley has noted, when administered a neuroleptic in high dosages, the psychotic's writing appears smaller like that of the Parkinsonism patient. And when Parkinsonism patients are given large amounts of L-dopamine, their handwriting takes on the larger, looser characteristics of the psychotic's writing.[4]

With such contrasting situations where both a drug and an illness can have the same effect, Matley admonishes that "If the writer is taking any medication or using any toxic substance, and if you do not account for that in your observations and interpretations, it is an odds on good bet that you are making a serious error in your opinion."[5]

When evaluating signatures of the elderly, the examiner must consider the possible effects of prescription drugs in addition to the individual's physical and mental condition. Medical records at or near the alleged date of signing may be necessary to obtain a clear understanding of what illnesses and/or medications may have impacted the person's writing abilities.

Regarding handwriting produced under the influence of drugs, it can generally be stated that stimulants cause size enlargements, sloppiness, carelessness, lack of continuity and letter forms, whereas depressants result in slower than normal writing, heavier pressure, a drawn appearance, deterioration of quality and unnecessary starts and stops.

In clinical trials conducted by several drug companies, of a total of 29 antidepressants 14 reportedly caused tremor. Antidepressants also have other side effects that are likely to influence handwriting as well. They include drowsiness, nervousness, dizziness, vertigo, anxiety, agitation, confusion, muscle stiffness, fatigue and panic.[6]

The influence of drugs and medications on one's script will depend on the drug, how much has been ingested, the subject's degree of tolerance, his or her physical condition, how long after taking the drug the

---

4. Marcel Matley, "Addiction and Handwriting-What Can You Tell?," The Vanguard, July-Sept., 1998, p.7.

5. Matley. *ibid.*

6. Joan Kastner & C. Dwight Townes, M.D., "Antidepressants and Their Effect on Handwriting," Journal of the World Association of Document Examiners, Vol. 214, No. 7.

person writes, and interaction with other medications or alcohol.

A study by Dhawan, et al.[7] showed that the time taken to copy a passage decreased under the influence of methamphetamine but increased under phenobarbitone. They discovered that the vertical dimension of writing increased under the stimulants caffeine and methamphetamine, but was not affected by the depressants chlorpromazine and phenobarbitone.

It appears that the individual's psychological makeup and stability influence the degree and direction with which the handwriting is apt to change following the use of drugs. It is reported that marijuana, for example, tends to increase the writing size and expansiveness of those users who are naturally more outgoing and expressive, while it tends to diminish the writing size of those who are more introverted, thoughtful and concentrated.

Handwriting experts, even if they also have medical or pharmacological training, should not expect to know all of the possible ways that drugs can affect writing. However, when faced with deteriorated writing it may be necessary for them to extend their investigation into the fields of health and medicine, particularly if they are aware that the alleged signer was ill or medicated at the time the signature was executed.

Highly recommended research guides in this regard are Drugs and Handwriting by Patricia Wellingham-Jones and Health and Handwriting, an Annotated Bibliography by Marcel Matley. With respect to specific drugs and illnesses, the Physicians Desk Reference is invaluable, as are visits to one's local medical or university library. There are thousands of articles that address the effect of medications on the body and many of them pertain directly to handwriting. On-line internet research will also prove helpful in this respect.

In no instance should the handwriting examiner attempt to discern specific illnesses or deduce the use of drugs based solely on the handwriting. Attempting any sort of diagnosis via the writing is unacceptable because it cannot be done with any certainty.

---

7. B. N. Dhawan, S. K. Bapat & V. C. Saxena, "Effect of Four Centrally Acting Drugs on Handwriting," Japanese Journal of Psychopharmacology, 1969, 19, pp.63-67.

External Influences

Frequently writing produced under adverse conditions comes under scrutiny as to authenticity. External factors or environmental influences that can cause writing to vary include writing position, surface and instrument, type of paper, available space and unstable writing conditions such as riding in a vehicle or writing on one's lap with a magazine for support.

Awkward writing positions generally result in less control of the pen. For example, when a person signs for a delivery the writing surface is sometimes suboptimal or unstable and/or the individual is balancing the package and signing at the same time.

Similarly, a person could be writing with the arm extended in order to reach over an object such as a hospital tray or a stack of papers. (See Figure 7.4.) Lack of support for the writing hand and decreased grip in these circumstances results in negative effects on the writing including decreased pressure, especially on upstrokes.

Awkward conditions reduce the precision of one's writing and, in many cases, cause it to appear carelessly produced. Nevertheless, one's usual writing habits show through, making the writing identifiable. Signatures or writing produced in odd positions are often more spread out so that any usual letter retraces may diminish and letters such as a and o will be open at the top rather than being formed in their normally closed fashion. There will likely be odd movements of the pen which result in poorly constructed loops or strokes that are longer than normal. The quality of the writing will also be variable so that some letters or words seem normal while others lack continuity.

Fig. 7.4—Normal writing (top) versus writing while reaching over a stack of papers with the paper at an angle (bottom). Note diminished pressure in bottom sample.

The position of the writing itself, rather than the writer's positioning, can also have an effect on the finished product. Signing in a small space or at the bottom of a page will possibly result in a reduction of size, but the basic writing features will not likely be altered appreciably since the writer's ingrained habits are not so readily changed.

The writing surface may influence the appearance of one's script, particularly if it is grainy, lumpy or indented. (See Figure 6.6 on page 85.) Certain writing media may also cause distortions in the writing ductus, as when the paper is especially rough. (See Figure 7.5.)

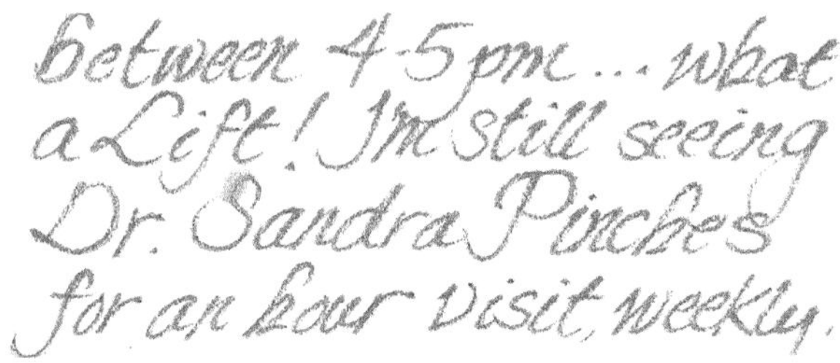

Fig. 7.5—Felt tip beveled pen on grainy paper.
Note rough appearance of strokes.

8. Comparison Standards

The availability of suitable and adequate comparison standards is likely the most important factor in formulating correct opinions in questioned document cases. Document examiners are constantly faced with the problem of adequate and legally verifiable standards (also referred to as exemplars) and they sometimes rely on insufficient material in reaching opinions.

When inadequate or improper exemplars are presented for examination along with the material in question, it is possible that the examiner will not be able to reach a solid conclusion. While it is generally up to the lawyer or client presenting the document problem to obtain the necessary comparison material, if the standards are unacceptable it is the examiner's responsibility to educate the client as to what is required to reach an unqualified opinion.

Legal Precedents

The admission of genuine writings in court for the purpose of comparison involves precedents which have evolved over many years. Attempts to develop a system of handwriting expertise started in Italy and France in the seventeenth century and by 1737 were incorporated into French law. But at that time no such expertise existed in the English speaking world.

Under the old English Common Law, experts of any kind did not play a large role in litigation. Even in those few instances when experts did offer testimony, they did so without a clearly defined set of legal principles to govern their qualifications or testimony.

The only kind of witness who could testify to the authenticity of writing under the old system was someone who watched the person perform the writing. Such a witness would testify to the specific act of writing, but not to the character, features or style of the disputed writing. Under this law it therefore served no purpose to suspect, or even discover, that a document was forged unless someone had actually witnessed the act. Even after writing comparison was finally allowed in legal proceedings, no standard writing could be admitted merely for comparison purposes; it had to already be in the case for some other purpose.

In 1854 the English Parliament enacted the Common Law Procedure

Act for the admission and comparison of handwriting in civil cases only. This allowed the expert or trier of fact to use exemplars "proved to the satisfaction of the judge to be genuine" for purposes of comparison. In 1865 the law was extended to apply to criminal cases as well.

In 1913 the United States passed a federal statute allowing the admission of genuine handwriting standards for comparison purposes. The statute reads (in part):

> In any proceeding before a court or judicial officer of the United States where the genuineness of handwriting of any person may be involved, any admitted or proved handwriting of such person shall be competent evidence as a basis for comparison by witnesses, or by the jury, court or officer conducting such proceeding, to prove or disprove such genuineness.[1]

Significance of Comparison Material

When working questioned signature or handwriting cases, the comparison standards should be the first material the examiner studies and questions, usually even before considering the suspect material, aside from anything that is immediately apparent with respect to the questioned writing. Questions should be raised about the exemplars produced, such as sufficiency, admissibility in court and certainty of authorship. Document examiner Edna Robertson writes that she is likely to question her clients more about the standards than the questioned writing and that she will not take a case if there is any uncertainty regarding the validity of the standards.[2]

The examiner should consider that when a client furnishes standards for comparison with a questioned writing, that person is hoping for an opinion favorable to his or her cause. It is not uncommon for clients to select writings that would appear to support their position and omit those that might prove damaging. A typical example is when an individual uses two or more signature styles depending on the type of document being signed. In an effort to prove or disprove authorship, they may produce comparison signatures of only the type that will support the conclusion they're seeking, while deliberately omitting those of the other style.

It is to be noted that signatures on cancelled checks, ordinarily

1. United States Code, Title 28, Section 1731.

2. Edna Robertson, *Fundamentals of Document Examination,* Chicago: Nelson-Hall Publishers, 1991.

deemed admissible for comparison, are not always written by the person whose name appears as the signature. Spouses often sign for each other, secretaries are authorized to sign for bosses and forgers sign for whomever. It behooves the examiner to exercise care and to pose questions to clients about the signatures presented in such cases.

In evaluating comparison material, the examiner is justified in questioning the client about the validity of the standards provided. *How does the client know the standards are valid? Can anyone else vouch for their authenticity?* If the client has not supplied an adequate number of standards written or signed during the right time period, the client should be given an explanation as to why such standards are necessary. The results from any document examination will only be as good as the material examined.

The document examiner is responsible for assuring that sufficient and appropriate standards are available to conduct an accurate comparison of writing. Unfortunately, it is often the attorney, the investigator or some other person interested in the questioned writing who selects and produces the writing specimens. Often that person is biased, has an agenda in mind or is not cognizant of the scope of the handwriting examination process.

In many cases the attorney or client does not know what is required by the document examiner in the way of comparison material and the examiner is often informed that the furnished standards are all that is available. If the comparison material is considered inadequate to successfully complete the assignment, additional documentation should be firmly requested. The search for standards should begin as soon as possible because in many instances time-consuming court action is required to make certain documents available, especially nowadays with more stringent laws pertaining to privacy issues.

Under most circumstances, normal course of business writing not produced specifically for the examination process is most desirable for comparison purposes. When such documentation is not available, it may be necessary to request writing from the suspect or suspects, as discussed below.

Legality of Standards

Comparison standards must be obtained legally. If they are not collected in a legal manner such as by subpoena, it is possible that the opposition will argue that they not be admitted into evidence at trial. Again, it is the responsibility of the attorney representing the examiner's client to consider this possibility. When working directly with a client and not through an attorney, care must be taken with regard to what the client produces for examination. Generally speaking, documentation produced during the normal course of business is considered acceptable for comparison, particularly if the signatures or handwriting thereon can be verified.

It is essential that when questioned signatures are involved, the exemplary signatures are valid. The examiner should not assume the suspect prepared the standards, no matter how logical that assumption might be. However, as noted above, the expert is often at the mercy of his or her clients with respect to what material is made available.

The judge hearing the case may rule to not allow any comparison documents or signatures to be placed into evidence unless the attorney proves them to be genuine. When dealing directly with clients rather than working through an attorney, the examiner may be given anything from old recipes to shopping lists to unsigned notes purportedly written by Uncle Bill or Aunt Mary. Anything that does not look official or that the client cannot legally verify should arouse suspicion. To reiterate, comparison material is often represented as valid in hopes of obtaining the answer the client is seeking. (Normally the examiner will state in the written report that his or her conclusions are based solely on the material supplied.)

How are signatures or handwriting proven valid so that they can be admitted into evidence as comparison standards? The best legal proof is the testimony of someone who witnessed the person perform the writing. Of course, many writing standards cannot be proven in this way.

To prove that standards are a part of permanent records used by an institution in the conduct of business, such as a bank signature card, the writer must be connected in some way with the record or with the institution and it must be shown that the documentation is in fact part of the writer's record. Testimony must be given to the effect that 1) a company employee supervised the preparation of the record, 2) such writings are regularly kept on file and referred to as specimen writings of this individual, and 3) the person who is presenting them has charge of their custody. (When a custodian of records produces documents in response to a subpoena, he or she is questioned under oath regarding such information as to their origin and his or her custody over them.)

Although far from the best proof and possibly even a dangerous proposition, it is possible in some courts to show that a specimen of writing was prepared by a particular individual through testimony of someone familiar with that person's writing. The rule here is that the proof of standard writing must satisfy the court. Appellate courts rarely overrule the lower court when such decisions have been reached.

Scope and Quality of Standards

Standards for comparison must be of good quality. Where possible, they should be original documents and not multi-generation copies or faxes. Documents bearing the comparison material should show no signs of deliberate disguise, alterations or changes.

Handwriting exemplars should be written at or near the same time as the questioned writing. Writing produced after the date of the questioned material may be deemed improper and inadmissible, particularly if it is suspected that the person created the writing specifically for the examination process to promote his side of the story.

Over the course of a person's lifetime, his handwriting may gradually change, just as physical appearance does. Writing or signature changes vary with each individual and can be subtle or quite drastic. Factors such as how much and how often the person writes should be considered, along with age, writing skill and mental and physical condition. Because signature changes are usually gradual (absent sudden illness or injury), material written within a two to three year range of the disputed writing should serve as satisfactory standards. However, as the lapse of years between the date of the standards and the date of the material under inquiry becomes greater, the standards are less likely to be representative.

It is possible for an individual's signature to undergo drastic changes in a very short period of time as when there is a serious illness or injury or when death is near. When a suspect will or other document is purportedly written when the testator is seriously ill or near death, signatures covering that time period are essential for comparison purposes. This is particularly so when the person is elderly.

Additionally, one must take into account the potential effect of medications. It would be wise to request from the client a list of any drugs the person may have been taking at or near the time of the writing in question. (In cases involving elderly people's signatures, the examiner is likely to be questioned during testimony about the issue of drugs and how they might alter one's writing or signature. The effect of awkward writing positions, such as being propped up on pillows or reaching over one's body to write while lying down, might also come under question.)

Exemplars should be in the same writing style or allograph as the questioned material. The examiner must compare printing to printing, cursive to cursive, numbers to numbers or signatures to signatures. The content should also be the same if at all possible, or at least similar. Onions cannot be compared to oranges with significant results other than they're both round.

If a signature is in question, signatures should be collected for comparison. If a check is believed fraudulent, genuine cancelled checks should be examined. If an account entry is in question, other similar entries will serve as the best standards. If medical records are at issue, medical records known to have been prepared by the suspect must be examined. The foregoing statements are not to imply that conclusions cannot be reached when the ideal criteria are not met, but they do represent the best case scenario with respect to comparison writing.

Ideally, the conditions under which the questioned writing was produced should be the same as the conditions under which the standards were written. The exemplars must show how the writer would likely produce the material in circumstances similar to those in which the suspect writing was prepared. A hastily written note would be a poor standard for comparison with material prepared in a formal setting. Unnatural writing positions introduce variations that make writing standards produced under these conditions less suitable for comparison with carefully written material. Writing specimens produced under unusual circumstances should not be depended upon exclusively for comparison with writing written under normal conditions, although they will serve as a valuable supplement to more optimal exemplars.

The writing instrument and paper utilized may also be important factors. For example, pen and ink writing contains characteristics that can generally not be discerned in pencil writing. Ballpoints produce writing that is not completely comparable to fountain pen writing. By its very nature, writing created with a felt tip pen is often thick and devoid of minute details and will therefore be relatively unacceptable as standards, unless the questioned writing was also written with a felt tip.

The size, shape, composition and ruling of paper may also affect the writing to a certain degree and sometimes writers adjust the size of their signatures to the amount of writing space available. Standards prepared on comparable paper or forms will be most reliable for the examination process.

Were all of the standards written by the same individual, or has the examiner been given one or more exemplar signatures that are non-genuine, perhaps authored by the person who executed the suspect writing? If the examiner is not alert to this possibility, the accuracy of his or her opinion may be distorted. It is imperative that the standards be arranged chronologically and that they be carefully compared one with another. If anything seems amiss with any of the exemplars, the client should be questioned thoroughly about the origin and authenticity of the questionable standard(s).

When collecting signature standards, it is important to consider the use for which each signature was written. Some writers have two or more distinct signature styles that they utilize for specific purposes, such as one style for checks, another for legal documents and still another for correspondence. The best exemplary signatures are those that were written for the same purpose as the signature in question. Without a collection of signatures written for various purposes, it is impossible to determine whether the writer employs more than one signature style.

There must be a sufficient quantity of standards in order to discern the natural variation in the handwriting of the author, and to determine the difference between such variations as opposed to someone attempting to simulate that person's signature. The standards should be numerous enough to reflect the individual writing habits of the person as such habits set him or her apart from all other writers.

There are no definite rules about the number of standards to be considered sufficient and the expert must often simply use his best judgment. James Conway states, "Signatures, like their authors, vary greatly in their complexities and accordingly there is no binding rule of number which will suffice or even be necessary in every case."[3]

A good general rule is the more comparison material, the better. One signature is certainly not enough, except under very rare circumstances. In most cases, 10 to 20 signatures should constitute an adequate sampling, although some problems may call for more and others can be solved with less. Much depends on the quality and character of the writing in dispute, meaning whether the alleged forgery is a skillful or clumsy imitation. When skillful simulations are in question, a larger number of standards are essential; with more clumsy forgeries, less comparative evidence is required to reach a conclusion as to inauthenticity.

Because it is more challenging to eliminate someone as a possible writer or signer of a document than it is to identify them, more comparison material is generally required to rule out a suspect.

Request Exemplars

When adequate handwriting from the suspect's normal course of business is not available, it may be necessary to request writing samples. It is important that the investigator procure request handwriting that is obtained legally and is as natural as possible.

The examiner should keep in mind that request writing may be considered self-serving evidence by the opposition. If a court action has already been filed, such self-produced standards are considered "post litem motam" and can legally be deemed inadmissible for the benefit of the maker of the exemplars. In such cases it is possible that they can be used by the opposition to prove their position. Consultation with the client's attorney is advised, but generally it is best not to request exemplars from one's own client unless the court so directs or the other party agrees.

The location for providing request writing samples may depend on opposing counsel. It is important that the process be witnessed and/or that the writing be notarized, as well as dated. All signature or writing samples should be numbered sequentially. The subject must initial or sign each exemplar provided and the witness must also sign each sample, or sign a statement that he or she witnessed the procedure.

When requesting handwriting exemplars for comparison purpos-

3. James Conway, *Evidential Documents,* Springfield, IL: Charles Thomas Publisher, 1959.

es, the suspect must duplicate the content of the questioned writing as closely as possible. Names, words, letters, letter combinations and numbers that appear on the questioned document must be obtained for accuracy of comparison. (The examiner might opt to use similar words from the questioned document, but in a different context. For example, if the word bitch appears in an anonymous note, the request material might include such words as itch, twitch or bewitched.) Instruction as to spelling, punctuation, spatial arrangement and so on is to be avoided.

The actual handwritten material in question must not be given to the suspect to copy. If he or she requests to see the document, it should be made available briefly, then promptly removed.

The suspect must write on paper of the same size and type as the document in question. If the questioned writing appears on a check, the sample should be written on the exact size of the questioned check; if the questioned document is a credit card charge slip, the writer must write on a paper that size, etc. Some banks provide "bank stock" checks which can be obtained upon request and used for this purpose. If these are unavailable, it is relatively easy to create mock-up checks.

Request exemplars should replicate the general layout of the document in question, including lines, spacing and margins. If the lines bearing the questioned writing are 2″ long and ½″ apart, the requested writing should be on lines 2″ long and ½″ apart. Where applicable, use unlined paper.

The writer should use the same type of writing instrument that was used on the questioned document. (Note that light-colored inks do not reproduce well and should therefore be avoided, especially if court exhibits will eventually be necessary.)

If the questioned document is handprinted rather than written in cursive, the suspect must print the exemplars, as handwriting cannot usually be effectively compared to handprinting. When signatures are in question, numerous signatures must be requested from the suspect. If numbers are at issue, several examples should be obtained.

Adhering to the following steps will help result in the collection of acceptable and useful comparison samples:

Step One. Seat the suspect comfortably and ask him or her to complete the Handwriting Questionnaire form offered at the end of this chapter. This form will elicit important information about factors which could have an influence on the writing samples, such as eyesight, handedness and medications. It will also provide general examples of letters, numbers and punctuation and will give the suspect a chance to "warm up" and relax.

Step Two. Allow the suspect to become more comfortable by writing the "London Letter" on the following page. The London Letter will furnish samples of each letter of the alphabet, both capital and lower-case. Ask the writer to produce this letter at least twice. In lieu of this, some innocuous material from a book or magazine may be dictated.

Step Three. Dictate the content of the questioned document, asking the suspect to write or print the material as described above. For shorter passages, several dictations are required, whereas with lengthy text less are acceptable. After the completion of each sample, remove that sample and have the suspect continue with the next. Request at least two samples of the same material in the writer's non-dominant hand.

Direct the suspect to sign his or her name at least ten times, making certain that the signature line is the same length as the signature line on the questioned document. If there is no signature line on the questioned document, do not provide a line. Have the suspect produce at least two signatures with the non-dominant hand. Ask the suspect to write three signatures in a standing position, and mark them accordingly.

If only signatures are required ask the person to write some text as well, in between producing the signatures. This prevents the signatures from being in a series. A continuous line of signatures down a page are of diminished value as exemplars because such a list may take on a character of its own. For example, the suspect may use disguise in writing the first signature and then continue the disguise by copying the signature on down the page.

If the suspect appears to write in an exceptionally labored way, insist that he or she produce continuous samples until a more natural writing speed is obtained. Laborious writing is often indicative of an attempt to disguise. (However, consider whether the writer is very ill, childlike or semi-literate or has some condition that could grossly affect the writing process.) Disguise will often show up as slow and uncertain movements, decreased fluency and rhythm, awkward letter formations, tremor, varying slant, exaggerated backhand and/or irregular baselines. If disguise is suspected, endeavor to obtain samples from another session at which time the writer will likely have forgotten the form of disguise used previously.

During the process of obtaining request writing samples, watch for signs of undue nervousness in the suspect which may be related to anxiety or guilt. Whether the suspect is innocent or not, he or she may be nervous simply because of having to give writing samples. This could cause the fluency of the writing to be adversely affected and might result in an artificial look. To get better cooperation, casual conversation and small talk can sometimes be employed to help put the suspect at ease.

If the suspect is to be questioned at the same session where writing exemplars are taken, it is usually considered best that the writing samples be obtained first; the questions may influence him or her in some way and could affect the writing.

Keep a master list of each exemplar and when it was completed, or simply note the start and end time at the bottom of the sheet of exemplars. During the procedure take note of any unusual occurrences, such as changes in attitude when writing certain information, a sudden shift of the writing instrument from one hand to the other, an awkward hold on the pen or, as noted above, very slow writing without a plausible explanation.

London Letter

Our London business is good, but Vienna and Berlin are quiet. Mr. D. Lloyd has gone to Switzerland and I am hoping for good news. He will be there for a week at 1396 Zermott Street. He then goes to Turin and Rome and will join Colonel Perry and arrive at Athens, Greece on Nov. 27th or Dec. 2nd. Letters there should be addressed: King James Blvd. 3580. We expect Chas. E. Fuller on Tuesday. Dr. L. McQuaid and Robt. Unger, Esq. left on the "Y. X. Express" tonight & paid $12.24 for tickets.

HANDWRITING QUESTIONNAIRE

FULL NAME ______________________________

ADDRESS ______________________________

BIRTH DATE ______________ BIRTH PLACE ______________

EDUCATION LEVEL __________ OCCUPATION ______________

1. Have you ever given handwriting samples for comparison purposes before? ____

   If so, explain: ______________________________

2. With which hand do you normally write? ______________

3. Can you write with both hands? ______________

4. Have you suffered any illnesses or injuries which may affect your writing? ____

5. Have you ever been treated for any alcohol or drug related problems? ______

   If so, explain: ______________________________

6. Are you currently under the influence of drugs or alcohol? ______________

   If so, explain: ______________________________

7. Are you currently taking any prescriptions or medications? ______________

   What kind? ______________________________

   Doctor's name ______________________________

   How often prescribed? ______________________________

   Time last taken ______________________________

8. Do you wear glasses? ______________________________

   Are you wearing them now? ______________________________

SIGNATURE ______________________ DATE __________

SIGNATURE ______________________ DATE __________

9. The Examination Process

The obvious purpose of conducting a handwriting examination is to arrive at logical conclusions regarding the matter at hand, based on the material presented.

The examiner has a direct responsibility in the outcome of the situation and must be able to adequately explain and/or demonstrate the reasoning behind any opinions that are deduced.

The comparison of handwriting is a gradual process that does not necessarily follow a steady progression in one direction. Because of the complexity of the process—due largely to the very nature and production of handwriting and the myriad of possibilities related to its execution—there can be no cut and dried approach. However, some practical considerations are presented here.

Procedures for working suspect writing cases vary somewhat according to the material involved and the questions posed. To a certain extent, each examiner will develop his or her own comparison methods. Whatever procedure is utilized, it is important to follow more or less the same system for every case in order to avoid errors and to show that one has a consistent, reliable methodology.

In every examination there must be complete objectivity and no reliance on personal feelings. Hunches based on experience with matters similar to the one at hand may prove valuable, but if and only if the examiner is able to find objective verification for those hunches. Also, information from clients should not be relied upon too heavily as it is often presented from a self-serving standpoint.

Preliminary Considerations

In working cases there is often a temptation to focus too extensively on the more obvious features of the writing. Fledgling examiners have a tendency to look first to individual letter formations without considering initially important matters pertaining to the handwriting or document that will help guide them to a more accurate investigation and analysis.

Valuable time and unnecessary work can be saved with some preliminary observations of the writing in question. For example, if the suspect writing is of high form level and written with apparently uninterrupted speed, suspects with naturally poor writing skills can be immediately eliminated. Or, if the questioned writing appears to be a tracing or simulation, it is a waste of time to attempt identification of the writer by examining numerous suspects' writing because their individual writing characteristics will have been suppressed by the copying process.

It is recommended that any questioned writing be read over thoroughly in order to familiarize oneself with the writer's style of expression, both from a linguistic standpoint and by way of letters, groups of letters, spacing and placement of sentences. This will give the reader-examiner an initial impression of the writer's overall style of expression and help identify what will be pertinent in the evaluation process. This approach is much like the connoisseur who appraises a painting and "knows" the artist's work from the creator's techniques, including the layout and perspective of the painting. With further consideration, he is able to tell fake from authentic based on the artist's individual style.

Where questioned signatures are at issue, it is often helpful for the examiner to imagine being the signer of the document by imitating the signature with a dry pen or reproducing it in the air. This affords a sense of the writer's rhythm, patterns of movement, connections and letter shapes.

Although valuable in the examination process, any initial impressions must be corroborated or disproved by further investigation. The examiner should make the following pertinent considerations before proceeding:

Does the writing in question appear to be naturally produced? If written fluently and with good line quality it is more likely genuine than if it has been poorly executed, barring of course the possibility of a genuine signature being "lifted" from another document and placed onto the new, false document. When a writing is created normally, its individual components may be readily accepted as the identifying features of its author, but if abnormally accomplished, every aspect must be carefully evaluated in light of its unusual or specific purpose.

Unnaturally executed handwriting can be evidenced by a "drawn" look, trembling or jagged strokes, contradictory signs of speed, variable slant, strong emphasis on the first portions of letters and words, uncharacteristic pen lifts or blunt finals.

However, conclusions in this regard must be substantiated by additional observations. With writing that is distorted, unnatural or unusual in any way, the examiner must consider if its condition may be due to the writing instrument or surface, disguise, physical or mental condition of the writer or circumstantial influences. Is it possible that the writing is a simulation or tracing, in which case its overall quality will likely be substandard?

Does the writing have any glaring errors? Do the mistakes seem innocent or are they perhaps deliberate?

Is the questioned writing of the same allograph or type as the standards (e.g., printing or cursive)? If not, an accurate evaluation is probably prevented as one writing type cannot normally be compared to another.

Examination Guidelines

Prior to the actual examination it must be determined that the comparison material is adequate and comparable, as suggested in Chapter 8. When the examiner is satisfied that an answer is possible based on the documentation presented, the questioned and known material must be organized and identified. First, all documentation is to be placed in chronological order. This is particularly important with regard to the comparison standards so that the examiner will be able to identify any changes in the writing over a period of time. Also, the timing of the signatures or writings may be significant to the issue. All questioned writing is to be identified as Q1, Q2, etc. and all known writing will be K1, K2, etc.

Once the material is in order, the questioned writing will be scanned at no less than 300dpi resolution into the computer, enlarged for ease of comparison and placed side-by-side with the known writing. In the case of signatures, the enlarged questioned signature can be placed at the top of the computerized worksheet, with the known signatures (enlarged to the same percentage) below, in order by date. The examination can then take place both on screen and in printed copies. The advantage of working on screen is that the material can be viewed at different magnifications.

Suggested Examination Protocol

Following a first-things-first approach, the examiner may choose to utilize the system presented below in evaluating questioned handwriting matters.

This procedure will lend stability to the expert's observations and aid in providing sound reasoning for any conclusions. To reiterate, each case must be handled individually according to its special circumstances. Additional document features, such as those presented in Chapter 2, should be evaluated as well.

The guide is to be followed in a step-by-step fashion, satisfying the first or lowest set of factors first before moving up to the next possible answer. Should sufficient explanation be discovered during preliminary steps, there may be no need to look further.

Mechanical and material factors. The initial investigation should include an evaluation of the nature and quality of the writing instrument and the materials used. Various writing tools have different qualities, papers are of varying degrees of texture, and the writing surface—desk, table, wall or notepad—may be rough, uneven, slick or indented. As suggested elsewhere, a defective pen may cause gooping or skips in the writing line. An uneven surface may result in jagged lines, skips of the pen, variable pressure or partial loss of control. Saudek notes that poor writing materials disrupt sentence impulse, distort the writing and generally diminish the comparison value of the written material.[1]

Skill level. If the writing is laborious, shaky, unnatural or distorted, it should be determined if the suspect has gained graphic maturity and, if so, whether he or she is familiar with the language being written. A writer of low skill level cannot produce the same skilled writing as the person with a higher graphic maturity level. Unfamiliarity with the language involved might also cause writing uncertainty and momentary interruptions in the writing process, except in the case of signatures which are apt to be more automatic.

Writing circumstances. The examiner should inquire as to the alleged circumstances under which a writing was produced, particularly if the writing is distorted or tremulous. Asking in advance can resolve many of the identification problems that might later be encountered, keeping in mind the possibility of deceit or bias on the part of the client. Adverse or unusual conditions can cause temporary changes to genuine writing. Whether the writer was standing at a counter, bending over, or writing while seated in a moving vehicle may make a difference in the overall

1. Robert Saudek, *Experiments With Handwriting*, New York: William Morrow and Company, 1929, p.291.

evaluation. Writing changes will also be evident if the person was lying down and/or reaching over his body while signing a document.

Health and physiological condition. As one's physical state can affect his or her writing, it is also to be considered. Effects of illness, drugs or medication, alcohol, fatigue, age or physical limitations such as an injured hand or arm, can cause a person's writing to differ from earlier samples. These conditions may be temporary or permanent and contemporaneous standards are especially important.

Psychological state. One's state of mind at the time of writing may have an influence on the handwriting and should therefore be considered. Anger, fear, emotional instability or anxiety can cause writing to vary momentarily, as can more positive states such as elation. However, such changes are likely to be minimal to the overall structure of the writing.

Deliberate pictorial effect. Some people adopt deliberate writing that lacks fluidity and spontaneity. This can be a calligraphic style, block lettering, a teenager's imitation of an admired script or the use of a very stylized "persona" writing that is more artistic or affected than natural. Any of these styles could be affectations or attempts at deliberate disguise.

Writing speed and impulse. Writing speed (fast, moderate or slow, regular or disrupted) and writing impulse (letter, word or sentence) lend clues as to naturalness. These features are to be compared between the questioned and known material for similarities or differences. Naturally slow writers and/or those of letter or word impulse, do not have the skill to produce sentence impulse writing. If letter impulse is utilized, are the frequent pen lifts due to limited skill, physiological problems, imitation (simulation) or disguise? Infrequent adjustments of the pen (as in sentence impulse) indicates concentration on the content of the writing rather than on how it was being written and, as such, is a sign of genuineness.

Line quality. The quality of the line will be a major indicator in the evaluation process, providing the examiner first considers skill level, writing speed, writing instrument and physiological influences as noted above. Minute hesitation points, pen lifts or careful retouching are primary signs of simulation, while free-flowing script of good line quality is one indication of genuineness. (See Chapter 6.)

Class characteristics. If the questioned and known writings are of obviously different classes, they were probably not written by the same person, unless that person knows both styles of writing, in which case other less obvious features will match. The same class characteristics in both writings certainly does not indicate common authorship. Similar class characteristics may classify a writer as belonging to or coming from a particular group, but will not identify that person.

Comparison of Specific Handwriting Features

Once the examiner has considered the possibilities above, the examination of more specific handwriting features can be pursued. Individual characteristics are to be studied, evaluated and assigned their proper weight, all the while using careful logic and observation. A scientific process of identification is established because the examiner uses analysis, comparison, evaluation, conclusion and, where possible, verification.

In evaluating these features, side-by-side comparison works most effectively. It is suggested that characteristics be copied by using a scanner and a page layout software program which allows for enlargement and placement of questioned material in juxtaposition with known. Any material can then be viewed on screen in various magnifications and in hard (printed) copy.

The comparison process can be facilitated by utilizing the worksheets at the end of this chapter. The examiner may wish to create similar computerized worksheets so that writing components can be scanned into the computer and placed into their proper categories.

As previously described in Chapter 4, the following writing features should be considered:

Arrangement—Margins, paragraph construction, alignment and overall placement of the written material on the page should be evaluated for similarities and differences. Arrangement habits are relatively fixed and usually not changed with disguise or unusual writing circumstances.

Size and Proportions—Size is not entirely reliable as an identifier because it is easily altered at will and may change in some instances, as with limited writing space. However, letter proportions are good identifiers as they remain relatively constant under most writing conditions, including disguise. Ratios remain even when overall writing size is altered. Ratios of upper zone formations compared to midzone letters are especially stable and potentially identifiable. Measurements should be made of the midzone, upper zone and lower zone and the ratios determined as instructed in Chapter 4.

Pressure—The pressure patterns of one's writing and signature (especially the latter) are relatively consistent. However, care must be taken as pressure can be temporarily changed at will. It may also vary with illness or other physiological concerns. The examiner must use caution when examining machine copied material for indications of pressure.

Spacing (line, letter, word)—Spacing patterns tend to remain consistent, even with changes in writing size. Extreme spacing patterns have more identification value than average spacing. Look for recurrent, unusually spaced letter combinations. Signature spacing patterns are particularly revealing and are often overlooked by the imitator. Measurement of line, letter and word spacing is discussed in Chapter 4.

Connecting strokes—Note length and degree of curvature, amount of angularity and any minute divergences in connections. Forgers often fail at properly reproducing connectors.

Hiatuses and pen lifts—Hiatuses can be significant as identifiers, as they are one indication of the writer's pen scope. Habitual breaks after or before certain letters will be important, except with capital letters. Simulation often requires that the person momentarily lift the pen to mark time, making hiatuses one indication of forgery. It must be determined that they are not related to interruption or accident. If care is taken to replace the pen at the exact point where it was lifted, it can be a verification of non-genuineness, especially with regard to elderly people who may be incapable of such exactitude.

Initial and terminal strokes—Tapered initial and terminal strokes point toward authenticity. Blunt initials and terminals are indicative of slow writing which may result from simulation or tracing. This must be verified, as blunt starts and stops occur naturally in some people's writing.

Embellishment and simplification—Embellishments may be used unconsciously and will possibly show up even in disguised writing. Embellishment or simplification of certain individual letters and not others will be helpful in identification.

Abbreviations—Largely unconscious characteristics are apt to appear in abbreviated words, especially on envelopes. Consider relative size of letters used in the abbreviation as well as punctuation, placement of apostrophes, alignment and spacing. They are often neglected by the person attempting disguise.

Slant—Slant is generally not a reliable identifying feature because it can be deliberately changed and may vary with circumstances. However, the slant pattern of one's signature, if consistent from one signing to another, may be an identifying or eliminating factor. (Slant pattern here means the relative slant of letters to one another.) Variable slant in a questioned writing, if not present in the standards, is a possible indication of simulation, but may also be caused by adverse circumstances such as a change in body position.

Punctuation, Diacritics—The formation, placement and alignment of these features are often useful in identification. They are sometimes omitted in simulated signatures, or placed too deliberately or in the wrong position, indicating a lack of natural flow of the writing trail.

Signs and Symbols—These formations have high identification value. Their slant, positioning, or spacing in relation to other characters may be significant. The ampersand may be especially revealing. Signs and symbols are frequently overlooked in disguise.

Spelling—This is not usually a strong identification feature, unless the misspelling is quite unique to a particular suspect. Be careful of commonly misspelled words or those misspellings attributable to dialect and mispronunciation.

Individual letters—It is suggested that numerous examples of each letter be examined in the writing in an effort to assess 1) potential uniqueness of letters in comparison to the writing model and 2) naturally varied forms of the same letter within the same writing. To be thorough, the examiner should work from *A* to *Z*, taking note of every way in which the writer forms each letter. Initial, medial and terminal positions of letters may affect their appearance and any variation or patterns of execution should be noted. Worksheets presented at the end of this chapter will be useful in this endeavor.

In shorter writings, consider the letter used most frequently. Which characteristics are consistent within the known writing? Which vary or appear only rarely? Are there any letters or formations in the writing that are especially unusual in any way which will help establish authorship?

In many cases it will not be necessary to examine every single letter of the alphabet, as identification or elimination will already have occurred somewhere higher up in the examination process. At this juncture, to be absolutely certain, less common letters such as q or z might be considered.

The comparison process can sometimes be facilitated by reviewing common words like the, and, from or to. Often these words are written with strong individuality, either in letter formation, alignment or spacing. Sometimes writers develop efficient ways of writing words they use frequently and these too are valuable identifiers.

Conclusions Based on the Examination

The principle of identification has to do with the comparison of similarities and differences between two or more handwriting samples and the proper evaluation of same.

The process is not merely a matter of comparing forms, but a more complex procedure calling for analysis, comparison and evaluation. Huber and Headrick present the three-part examination process as:

1. *Analysis*—The known and unknown are reduced to properties and characteristics that can be directly observable, measurable or otherwise perceptible.

2. *Comparison*—Properties and characteristics of the unknown, determined through analysis, are now compared with the known properties or characteristics.

3. *Evaluation*—Similarities and differences in properties or characteristics each have a certain value for identification, based on likelihood of occurrence. The weight or significance of each must therefore be evaluated.[2]

Failure to reach an opinion of non-identity when one is justified may involve a failure in either the analysis or evaluation stage. During the analytical part the examiner must decide on the basic qualities of the questioned and known writings, such as whether there is evidence for disguise or simulation. Failure during the evaluation stage typically en-

2. Roy Huber & A. M. Headrick, *Handwriting Identification: Facts and Fundamentals*, New York: CRC Press, 1999.

tails lack of assignment of proper weight to differences.[3]

When two writings or signatures are roughly similar, there are three possible explanations. Either they were produced by the same person, they match by chance, or the writing in question is a good simulation that cannot be detected.

The likelihood of a chance match is remote when the examiner has access to enough exemplary material to accurately determine range of variation and when the writing being examined is of sufficient quantity. Logically, it is easier to simulate or disguise a small amount of writing than a longer passage, meaning more of a chance that two writings will be incorrectly determined to be of common authorship. It is the examiner's task to conclude whether any similarities between writings are both sufficient and uniquely characteristic enough to be deemed from the same writer.

When writings are generally dissimilar, more possibilities must be taken into account. Disparities may indicate different writers, but the examiner must consider potential disguise or the possible adverse effect of internal influences (illness, drugs, nervousness) or external influences (defective writing tool, rough surface). It may also be possible that a writer simply has more than one writing style.

Normally there are many or perhaps several differences between the handwriting of two people, even if they are similar pictorially. When dissimilarities are evident, it is important to determine whether the differences are consistent and not attributable to chance or accident. If so, the two writings were authored by two people.

In most instances it is more challenging to eliminate than identify a writer because there are more possibilities to consider such as a suspect's wide range of natural variation of which the examiner might be unaware. If a questioned writing exhibits features that are beyond the natural variation evidenced in the known writings, one cannot be certain that additional exemplars might also exhibit those features apparent in the questioned writing. Essentially, there is more ground to cover when attempting to eliminate a suspect.

In all cases it is important to obtain reasonable amounts of relatively contemporaneous comparison material so as to establish writers' natural variation. Otherwise, there is the danger of reaching incorrect conclu-

3. Jan Beck, "Sources of Error in Forensic Handwriting Evaluation," Journal of Forensic Sciences, Vol. 40, No. 1, Jan. 1995.

sions.

In identifying or eliminating suspects, the fundamental features of writing must be taken into account. By way of definition, fundamental features are those basic structures that create meaningful form and identify a handwriting as belonging to one person. Habit dictates that such features are automatically repeated in a similar way within words or sentences that have the same letter groups or configurations.[4] Fundamental differences are those structural deviations that distinguish one writing from another.

A structure or formation that appears in one writing but in none of the other writings under examination would not classify as normal variation, but would be considered fundamentally different from the other writings. In every case the number, nature and quality of any similarities or differences must be carefully considered. In rare instances, one or two unusual features may in and of themselves be positive identifiers. Usually, however, conclusions are based on numerous points of similarity or difference, the cumulative evidence.

Identification

To identify a writer, one must establish sufficient similarities not attributable to chance or accident. Additionally, there can be no unexplainable fundamental differences.

If all letter forms in a questioned writing or signature have a structural resemblance to the standards, any disparities cannot be classified as being fundamentally different. It will be important of course to have sufficient comparison standards to reach this conclusion.

If even one or two exemplars are sufficient to prove authorship, then variability in any additional exemplars cannot negate the conclusion of identity, providing there are no problems with the exemplars.

When delicate, inconspicuous parts of a writing are executed consistently on repeated occasions, and especially if they are written freely, it is safe to conclude that they are elements that are not disguised.[5]

---

4. Edna W. Robertson, *Fundamentals of Document Examination*, Chicago: Nelson-Hall Publishers, 1991

5. Huber & Headrick, *ibid.* p. 279.

Elimination

When different structural features in a writing cannot be accounted for by reason of occasional habit, writing conditions, physiology, accident or other reasonable causes, the examiner must reach a conclusion of different writers.[6]

Harrison states that "whatever features two specimens of handwriting have in common, they cannot be considered to be of common authorship if they display but a single consistent dissimilarity in any feature which is fundamental to the structure of the handwriting, and whose presence is not capable of reasonable explanation."[7]

The examiner must take care in determining uncommon authorship because, as Harrison points out, differences between writings must be fundamental to the structure of the handwriting and not merely variations or the result of accident.

When differences occur in spontaneous writing, they have more value in proving uncommon authorship than when they appear in deliberate, possibly disguised or simulated writing.

In proving different authors, disparities between writings need not be obvious. In fact, dissimilarities that are inconspicuous are apt to have more value, considering that it is possible to consciously introduce disparities, as in disguise. Again, if the structural basis of the writing is involved, the opinion of two writers is corroborated.

As explained more thoroughly in Chapter 10, indications of falsity may include gross or muscular tremor (evidencing slow writing), awkward letter forms, lack of fluidity in writing movement, disrupted rhythm, pauses while writing, blunt terminals, unvaried pressure and changeable slant.

Often questioned and known writings bear strong resemblances to one another at first look. Examiners are sometimes overly influenced by similarities between writings so that they do not see any disparities and then fail to eliminate writers. This may occur in instances where the questioned and known material belong to the same class of writing as in the case of foreign writings that are unfamiliar to the examiner, or the "bubble writing" common to teenage girls. One must be astute in looking at similarities and not ignoring what is different. Once a significant

---

6. Robertson, *ibid.*, p. 146

7. Wilson Harrison, *Suspect Documents,* Chicago: Nelson-Hall Publishers, 1981, p.343.

dissimilarity is noted and attention is drawn away from the close resemblance of the two writings, other disparities are often readily observed.

If there are sufficient significant and unexplainable differences to create a reasonable probability that a suspect is not the author, then any similarities, whatever their number or import, cannot lead to an identification. Consider the fact that in order for a simulated signature to pass as genuine, it must at least look like it is genuine and it will therefore have some apparent similarities with that which is authentic.

Albert Osborn, one of the founding fathers of handwriting and document examination, stated, "If even a few qualities are distinctly foreign to the genuine writing, or are violations of the fixed habits in the genuine writing, and cannot be explained in any reasonable manner, then the conclusion must be that the writing is not genuine."[8]

---

8. Albert Osborn, *The Problem of Proof,* Albany, New York: The Boyd Printing Company, 1946, p.484.

Comparison Worksheet

Feature	Questioned	Known
Arrangement		
Size		
Proportions (UZ:MZ:LZ Ratio)		
Pressure		
Spacing, line		
Spacing, letter		
Spacing, word		
Connecting strokes		
Hiatuses/Pen lifts		
Initial, Terminal strokes		
Embellishment, Simplification		
Abbreviations		
Slant		
Punctuation		
Signs, Symbols		
Spelling		
Additional Observations		

Individual Letter Comparison Chart

	Questioned				Known		
	Init.	Mid.	Term.		Init.	Mid.	Term.
Aa							
Bb							
Cc							
Dd							
Ee							
Ff							
Gg							
Hh							
Ii							
Jj							
Kk							
Ll							
Mm							
Nn							
Oo							
Pp							
Qq							
Rr							
Ss							
Tt							
Uu							
Vv							
Ww							
Xx							
Yy							
Zz							
0							
1							
2							
3							
4							
5							
6							
7							
8							
9							

10. Signature Evaluation

In many questioned writing cases it is the signature on the document that is at issue with regard to authenticity.

The signature is generally a person's most common writing act and, as such, is largely habitual. As there are essentially no rules with respect to devising and producing signatures, they are open for being highly individualized according to each person's mental design.

Often deliberately formulated, the person's signature serves as a "trademark." Signatures can be written as tangled, illegible shapes or a series of clearly decipherable letters that distinctly spell out the person's name. In many cases they have no resemblance to the writer's name at all, but are merely identifying marks. One's signature may include extraneous marks, appendages or dots.

In any case, their construction and execution are relatively stable and their features more or less subconsciously produced. Due to their repetition, writing strokes and formations that comprise a person's signature are generally consistent, even over long time spans. It is the combination of personal attributes, writing form and quality—all habitual—which identifies one's signature as authentic.

Of course no one ever signs identically the same from one time to another. There are some variations from signature to signature due to temporary effects of either an instrinsical or extrinsical nature, but their overall construction remains intact. This makes signatures highly identifiable, assuming proper standards are available for comparison.

It is not uncommon for an individual to utilize two or more signature designs depending on the type of document being signed. There may be one type for business letters, another for personal correspondence and yet another for more formal occasions such as signing important documents like legal papers. In some cases the writer might sign a first and last name while other instances call for the inclusion of the middle name as well. Sometimes only initials suffice. Nowadays, printed signatures are becoming more common.

With those who are illiterate, a cross mark serves as an identifying mark when affixed to a document, in which case the word *His* or *Her* is normally written above the *X* and the word *Mark* below. Such marks are challenging forensically, usually due to insufficient comparison material. Nevertheless, there will be consistency in writing speed, pressure, alignment and balance of the mark as well as length and positioning of the two cross bars.

Although questioned signatures probably make up the bulk of most handwriting examiners' workload, falsified signatures pass as genuine every day. The layperson, if taking time to consider whether a signature being presented might be inauthentic, is apt to note only its pictorial appearance and not the significant details that determine genuineness. Store clerks performing credit card transactions take a cursory look at signatures on customers' identification, if at all. Even bank tellers who see a multitude of signatures in their daily work are generally unaware that authenticity goes deeper than initial impressions.

Forgers, also generally unaware of the nuances of writing, often focus on the obvious features of the signature being simulated such as the capital letters, slant and loops, qualities that make an immediate impression and usually allow the phony signature to pass as genuine.

In general, signatures are made up of a somewhat limited amount of letters or shapes. For writers who sign their names frequently, signatures are particularly automatic and generally fluent. For those who sign less often, it is possible that signing may be more of a conscious effort, possibly with evidence of a lower skill level and less freedom of movement. The degree of normal fluency exhibited by a person's signature will be evidenced by the comparison material collected.

A study of a collection of a writer's known signatures reveals that person's personal design and whether they are executed with smoothness and continuity of movement or, on the other end of the spectrum, with halting strokes, tremor and/or pen lifts. As suggested elsewhere, good line quality and unbroken movements are signs of genuineness, providing the person's normal signatures are also reflective of the same qualities.

Therefore, in determining the validity of signatures, some of the first features to consider are movement, line quality and fluency. Are the strokes of the signature continuous, or do lifts of the pen occur at various intervals? If there are lifts, do they appear to be in natural places such as between letters? If any unnatural pen lifts are apparent, then it must be determined whether they are the result of simulation related to the forger's uncertainty or due to circumstances surrounding the writing.

When retouching is evident, the examiner must look closely at the patched areas to see if they are the product of the forger's attempt to make the signature "perfect," always a vital mistake. When and if an error is made in a genuine signature and the person chooses to correct it, the correction is apt to be done obviously, unlike the forger who carefully rectifies any slip-ups to avoid arousing suspicion. Microscopic examination of such patching can be especially revealing.

When signing a document the person is normally concerned about the contents and meaning of the paper being signed, rather than on the mechanics of the signing process. Consequently, the signature is likely to appear natural and non-deliberate. If not, suspicion should be aroused.

Genuine signatures are usually written with a certain rhythm and a rate of speed typical of the writer. Beginning and terminal strokes are written smoothly and generally with tapered starts and finishes. Connections between letters are apt to flow smoothly and there is a "naturalness" evident in the firmness of stroke, the pattern of shading or emphasis, and the habitual movements of the writing. In most cases each name or segment of the signature will flow naturally into the next.

Nongenuine signatures are often defective in that the rhythm and natural flow are disrupted, signs of the forger's inability to correctly execute movements that are foreign to his or her usual style. Such signatures are sometimes hesitant and may take on a jerky or tremulous appearance. In especially poor simulations, they may seem labored or drawn. They sometimes look disjointed, with angled instead of rounded curves and connections. There will possibly be blunt beginning and ending strokes reflective of pauses in the writing act.

Suspect signatures are normally deemed authentic when they are similar to the known signatures in pictorial style, form or design, movement, connections, proportions and alignment. They must also be of the proper rhythm and line quality, barring the possible influence of adverse writing conditions and/or health or medication issues.

This of course eludes to the possibility of anomalies in genuine writing. As Charles Scott has stated, "Genuineness and perfection are not synonymous; certain defects are often found in signatures that are unmistakably genuine."[1]

1. Charles C. Scott, *Photographic Evidence,* Kansas City, MO: Vernon Law Book Company, 1942.

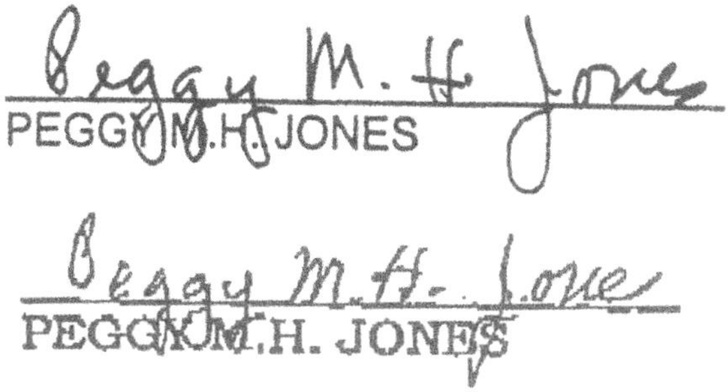

Fig. 10.1—Genuine signature (top) versus nongenuine signature (bottom)

In considering the veracity of questioned signatures, it is imperative to obtain and carefully examine adequate and comparable genuine signatures in order to determine the writer's natural variation. As further discussed in Chapter 8, there must be a sufficient number of exemplary signatures that are relatively contemporaneous with the material in question and produced under various conditions and for different purposes.

The degree of natural variation will vary with individual writers as well as the prevailing circumstances at the time each signature was written. Some have considerably variable signatures while others write with exceptional consistency. In general, rapidly produced, spontaneous writing indicates the likelihood of a wide range of variation, making it doubly important to procure numerous known signatures for the comparison process. Those who write slowly and deliberately are apt to have more controlled and therefore more consistent signatures, making for less natural variation and not as much need for extensive exemplars.

When reviewing a series of genuine signatures the examiner directs attention toward discovering which of the signature elements are the most individual or unique and therefore are of greater evidential value. Attention should be given to any elements of the signature that vary remarkably as well as those that do not change appreciably from one signing to another.

The examiner's skill level and degree of experience will determine how critically signatures are compared and their similarities and differences comprehended. As Hagen stated, "The measure of accuracy which may be reached as to the genuine or forged character of a signature…will depend upon the ability of the examiner to ascertain and determine the physical habit of the writer by the details appearing in the writing produced by it."[2]

In identifying an individual as the writer of a signature in question, there must be sufficient significant similarities between the questioned and known material and the absence of any unexplainable differences. No one or two features can be relied upon to make an identification, as it is the combination of all of a signature's elements that mark it as authentic.

If, after establishing the writer's range of variation, it is determined that the signature in question contains features that are not within that range, then the examiner must ask if it is even possible for the writer to create those non-matching features. If so, then he or she must consider the possibility that the comparison material may not have been sufficiently extensive to reveal those particular elements.

One must also look at the possibility of accidentals. In such instances there will likely be some minimal difference of one or two aspects while the rest of the signature in question matches the known.

If there are structural differences between the questioned and known signatures that cannot otherwise be explained, then the signatures are of uncommon authorship. Fundamental or significant differences are often inconspicuous movements or formations that do not fit into the scope of the writer's natural variation. They are primarily unconscious elements such as pressure patterns, method of joining strokes, non-apparent tics or hooks, specialized movements, spacing patterns, proportional elements or alignment. In short, they are those aspects of the writing that are particularly individual which the forger either overlooks or cannot accurately reproduce.

Even a single fundamental difference between signatures denotes inauthenticity. However, the examiner needs to consider whether sufficient exemplars have been studied before reaching that conclusion. In most cases of forgery multiple differences are apparent, obviously increasing the evidence for an opinion of non-genuineness.

2. William E. Hagan, *A Treatise On Disputed Handwriting*, New York: Banks and Brothers, 1894, p.36.

Initials

Like signatures, initials identify their authors. Handwriting examiners are often approached with questions regarding documents that have been initialed where choices or changes have been acknowledged or mistakes corrected. Forms of all types are often initialed, usually as a sign of agreement, and inter-office memos are initialed in place of full signatures. Individual pages of wills are normally initialed by the testator, which initials are sometimes questioned in conjunction with, but sometimes apart from, the document's signature(s).

Initials generally consist of one or more of the first letters of the person's name. They are usually written as one connected unit, but are sometimes placed separately. Some are followed by dots, others circled and still others underlined. In most cases they are written rapidly.

Harrison notes that "many people who write normally in other respects initial documents with a group of closely entwined, floridly written capitals."[1] He indicates that these formations are easily forged because it will generally suffice to simply create the outlines of the initials without being concerned about minor writing details. Harrison is correct that forging initials is generally a relatively easy task given the small amount of writing to master. Certainly, they are easier to forge than are entire names.

In most cases initials cannot safely be compared to signatures or other writing. Sometimes one or more of an individual's initials will be formed like the same letters of his or her signature, but often they are not. In fact, the overall individual characteristics of the signature may be quite dissimilar to the features that comprise one's initials. And capital letters of a person's cursive writing are frequently different in style than those of the initials, making them also generally unsuitable for comparison.

Like other handwriting, initials are identifiable due to their specific formations and features and their examination is therefore carried out in similar fashion as other handwritten material. However, the challenge in identifying or eliminating writers of initials includes relatively little questioned material and the likelihood of limited comparison standards. Success in this respect also involves the degree of complication with which the initials are formed and interconnected.

1. Wilson Harrison, *Suspect Documents*, Chicago, Nelson-Hall Publishers, 1981, p.413.

Fig. 10.2—Initials versus signature. Note few similarities.

Forged Signatures

There are three basic types of signature forgery—simple forgery, freehand simulation and tracing.

Simple forgeries

Simple forgery involves writing another person's name without any attempt at imitating the signature. This type of forgery may be used when an individual's identification is stolen and the perpetrator of the forgery relies on the store clerk or bank teller's negligence in checking the I.D. These forgeries can usually be spotted easily as the writing will appear natural and the questioned and known signatures will show very different writing habits. In most cases, with exemplary signatures produced by the forger he or she can be identified as the writer because there is no attempt at using an unaccustomed writing style or hiding one's usual writing features.

Freehand simulations

Freehand simulation of signatures is probably the most frequently used method of forging signatures. With this approach the forger makes an attempt to copy a genuine signature, usually by keeping the signature in front of him while trying to reproduce it. This entails shifting one's eye back and forth between the original and the forgery which tends to result in hesitation, inaccurate lines and/or distortions. Essentially, these signatures are more drawings than writings. Some forgers take time to practice simulating a signature until it begins to feel more familiar and natural. Rehearsed simulations are apt to be somewhat more smoothly executed, but in most cases will still show evidence of uncertainty or movements that are not consistent with the genuine signature.

When attempting a freehand recreation of a signature the forger is faced with two major simultaneous tasks—adopting writing movements that are unfamiliar and suppressing his own writing habits. In taking on alien writing movements, he must accurately reproduce the correct rhythm and flow of the genuine writing, the right pressure and shading patterns, slant, direction of movement, size and proportions, initial and terminal strokes and connectors, not to mention properly shaped individual letters.

This arduous task was accurately depicted in the movie Dead Ringer in which Bette Davis plays twins. One of the twins murders the other and takes over her identity in order to "inherit" her lavish lifestyle and estate. This naturally required that she learn the murdered sister's signature in order to execute legal and financial documents. However, even with practice the impostor was finally unable to accomplish the task. As a last resort, she burned her writing hand with a hot fireplace poker which then afforded her the excuse of signing with her non-dominant hand.

Success in capturing subtleties of a signature depends on the forger's skill level and the nature of the signature being recreated. Contrary to the layperson's general belief, a carefully written, clearly legible signature with no curlicues or fancy movements is the most difficult to simulate. On the other hand, a tortuous, twisted signature comprised of illegible formations can be more readily depicted, at least well enough that the forgery may pass as genuine.

Basically, when a forger simulates a writing he must choose between writing fast (which produces generally better line quality but a less accurate reproduction) and slower writing (which results in a more accurate copy of letter forms but a loss of line quality).

Classic indicators of simulated signatures include:

- Slowly executed letters and shapes
- Poor line quality
- Uncertain, interrupted lines

- Wavering strokes (gross or muscular tremor)
- Blunt starts and stops
- Unnatural pen lifts
- Pen rests
- Touched up letters
- Marked variation of slant
- Disproportionate letter sizes and loops

It must first be ascertained whether any of the above-noted features are evident in the genuine signatures as well.

It is often not possible to identify the creator of a forged signature due to the fact that that person's own writing habits have necessarily been squelched. Exceptions are simple forgeries as noted above or signatures where the victim and forger both have the same last name. In the latter instance the forger sometimes inadvertently slips back into his habitual name writing patterns so that the surname of the forgery is remarkably similar to his own. Armed with request exemplars where the suspect is required to reproduce the signature in question, the examiner may be successful in identifying the forger.

Tracings

A rather common way to forge signatures is by tracing. The examiner should be alert to this possibility when reviewing questioned material, particularly when two or more signatures presented for the examination are remarkably similar. In some instances the genuine signature that was traced may even be presented as an exemplar to prove the authenticity of the signature in question. In other cases more than one questioned signature will match each other in almost every respect, an indication that they were all produced from the same model.

Cases involving traced writing can be elusive when the model signature from which the tracing was created is unavailable. In this case it is likely that the disputed signature will be determined to be nongenuine, but it may be difficult to prove the signature was traced unless the original is carefully examined and there are signs of indentations or residue resulting from the carbon copy tracing procedure described below.

Basically, tracings are drawn reproductions taken directly from the original. They often have a deliberate appearance because the writing hand is not moving freely across the paper. In nearly every case the signature will evidence gross tremor which relates to inferior line quality. Generally, pressure is heavy and/or non-variable and shading of strokes is absent.

There are four essential methods that can be utilized to trace signatures:

1. Use of transmitted light with the genuine signature below and the new, false document placed on top of it so that the signature lines can be copied. This is the easiest method of tracing. Use of transmitted light (either up against a window or on a light table) allows the forger to see the outline of the signature below so that it can be readily traced over. This makes for the most skillful tracing, but because it requires considerable concentration the newly created signature will lack fluidity and good line quality. Essentially, it will appear drawn and heavy.
2. Tracing heavily over a genuine signature in order to leave an impression of the signature on the document below. Once the impression of the signature is accomplished, the forger then writes over the impression, carefully following the lines. This method is rather difficult and the signature will likely appear even more uncertain than with the transmitted light method. Microscopic examination of the original questioned signature and/or use of oblique lighting will likely reveal the indentations.
3. Use of carbon paper under a genuine document to create an image of the signature on the new document. As with method number two, once the carbon image is on the new document it is merely written over after which there may be an attempt to erase the still visible carbon. Under the microscope any traces of carbon will likely be seen and there is apt to be a halo effect on the outline of some of the strokes of the signature where the forger was not exact in following the lines. If an attempt was made at erasing the carbon traces, some of the signature's ink may have been smeared or eradicated, or the paper's fibers may have been disrupted.
4. Use of pin pricks to outline the signature. In this rather uncommon method the forger pens in the signature by following the tiny holes created by the pin point. It is unlikely that an accurate reproduction will be accomplished and the pin holes will be obvi-

ous in the new document.

Two signatures that are closely similar in nearly every detail are indicative of tracing. (This clue will of course exist only when the model signature is available.)

Tracings can be further identified by the following:

- Matching the questioned signature with the genuine. (Superimposing the signatures over a light table or creating a transparency of one and then positioning it over the other will help to accomplish this.)
- No variation between the questioned and known
- Constant, heavy pressure
- Blunt initial and terminal strokes
- Slight deviation in line direction perhaps accompanied by pen lifts
- Abrupt starts and stops of the pen
- Ink blotches indicating pen rests
- Corrections or retouching of strokes, sometimes subtle, sometimes written in the wrong direction

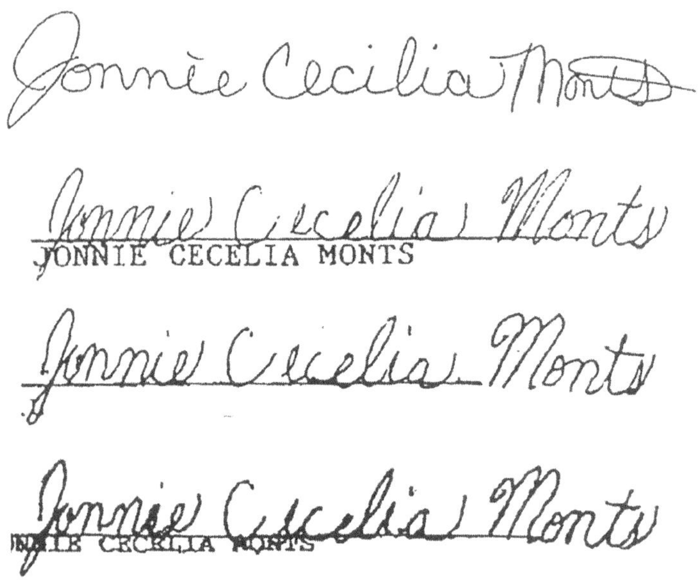

Fig. 10.3—Evidence of tracing. Signature 1=genuine. Signature 2=poor simulation of the genuine signature. Signature 3=tracing of signature 2. Signature 4=tracing of signature 3. Note progressive degeneration of line quality.

In examining a signature that is the product of tracing, there is no use attempting to determine who may have created the forgery. Drawing the signature's shape prevents any of the forger's own writing characteristics from surfacing.

11. Anonymous Writing

Anonymous writing is defined as any form of written communication in which the writer chooses not to acknowledge authorship. This might involve handwriting, printing, drawings, typewriting, or a combination of any of these. It might be a note, a letter, a message on a public building, or even words scrawled on a body.

Anonymous writers are motivated by any number of reasons, but usually have negative intent. They may be "normal, momentarily abnormal, or subject to irresistible impulses."[1] While many anonymous writings come from uneducated or naive people, they are not limited by age, social status, or education. In short, anonymous writings come from various people with sundry backgrounds and for different purposes.

An ex-girlfriend or ex-wife may seek revenge on a former significant other or the new spouse-to-be; a disgruntled employee may surreptitiously attack a superior or co-worker; a criminal may seek ransom money or attempt to blackmail the letter's recipient; a husband or wife may write spiteful anonymous notes to their partner, perhaps about disagreeable characteristics of the other's parent(s).

Although some anonymous writing serves beneficial purposes, most such material is designed to hurt or cause ill will. When the intent is negative, the missive is often referred to as a "poison pen letter." The anonymous writing may be as innocent as a practical joke or as serious as a letter bomb. Oscar Mendelsohn writes, "Because human spite and the wish to wound can arise from any cause or from no real cause at all, there is no limit to the subject and content of a poison-pen letter."[2]

Literature on the subject of anonymous writing seems to indicate that the majority of anonymous writers are women, except in the case of graffiti, which tends to be done more commonly by males. Mendelsohn indicates that silly and non-threatening notes are written primarily by women[3] and Baker reports that women seem to write more vicious and vulgar letters than men, using obscene language and profanity as

---

1. J. Newton Baker, *Law of Disputed and Forged Documents*, Charlottesville, VA: The Mitchie Company, 1955.
2. Oscar Mendelsohn, *Suspected Documents and Outrageous Liars*, Melbourne: Thomas Nelson Publishers, 1976.
3. Mendelsohn, *ibid.*

a disguise. (In practice, most anonymous writers *are* female, and they frequently employ equally crude and vulgar language and drawings as their male counterparts.) Baker also indicates that women frequently accuse innocent persons of their own sex, while men tend to write anonymously regarding business-related matters.

Occasionally, anonymous writers are well intentioned. A benefactor to a charitable organization, for example, might want to remain unnamed. But usually the anonymous writer is perpetrating some sort of unpleasant deed.

Types of Anonymous Writings

As suggested, anonymous writing appears in various forms and for many reasons. Sometimes the anonymous writer simply wishes to impart information, either positive or negative, to the recipient. Occasionally, letters or notes are written by well-wishers or secret admirers. Typically innocent notes of this type often show up around Valentine's Day. Usually, due to their benign character, such well-intentioned writings are not brought to the handwriting analyst for examination and, since these writers normally have honorable intentions, they have no reason to create a disguise and will typically write in their natural style, making for ease of identification when and if the analyst is consulted.

Anonymous writing is often designed to hurt. The writer may wish to take revenge on the recipient for a perceived or actual wrong-doing. The letter may be designed as a false accusation or a wish to tarnish the reputation or character of the recipient or someone close to the recipient. The writer's motivation may be a desire to humiliate. The writer could be a rejected lover with overpowering jealousy and hatred for the person now favored, or he might be an envious colleague venting not-so-professional jealousy.

Many anonymous communications are not particularly violent in tone, but are transmitted to cause irritation or annoyance. However, letters that are obviously threatening require immediate attention and should involve the authorities. (However, in my experience, the police are often reluctant to take action in such cases, perhaps due to legal ramifications or simply that they have more pressing matters that require their attention.) The most dangerous anonymous missives are of course those which contain explosive devices.[4]

4. Bruce B. Koffler, "Evidence in Letter Bombs and Parcel Bombs," International

Sometimes anonymous writing is borne of emotional or mental imbalance. Psychotic writers are quite easily recognized by their tangled and haphazard handwriting style and their incomprehensible choice of words. Letters from psychotics "usually lack coherence, continuity, intelligence, and consistent purpose" and they may emphasize unreasonable and ridiculous ideas.[5] It does not require a person trained in mental health to get the gist of their often strange symbols and highly bizarre individual letter formations.

When sexual preoccupation or problems underlie the perpetrator's actions, the writing may be accompanied by obscene language and/or drawings. And, contrary to what one might expect, sexual drawings and dirty language are by no means limited to males.

Frequently criminal intent is involved, as in the case of bank robberies where a note is passed across a counter demanding money. Police departments worldwide deal with such matters on a daily basis, utilizing the notes as evidence in an effort to establish authorship and ultimately convict the perpetrator.

Blackmail, extortion or ransom notes are used to add coercion in an attempt to obtain money or other goods, often in exchange for something highly valued by the victim. The writers of these letters are usually not satisfied with their first attempts, sometimes due to their eagerness and sometimes due to the initial lack of response to the demands. With blackmail, extortion and ransom attempts, the handwriting is generally disguised, but numerals are frequently written more naturally and in the habitual manner of the writer, sometimes enough to lead to identification.

Investigating Anonymous Writing

Whatever the intent of the writer, anonymous writing cases are generally disagreeable and difficult in nature, and they require careful and thorough investigation. It is suggested that the investigator have specific training in document examination before proceeding in order to avoid misidentification or potential legal problems arising from improper reports. If you are not trained specifically to handle questioned document

---

Journal of Forensic Document Examiners, Vol. 2, No. 2, April/June 1996, pp. 117-143.

5. James Conway, *Evidential Documents*, Springfield, IL: Charles C. Thomas Publisher, 1978.

problems, you would be wise to inform your potential client that you are only qualified to render a preliminary opinion.

If possible, the investigator should coordinate his or her efforts with an attorney. If the person seeking information about the anonymous writing is not represented by legal counsel, you might suggest that he retain an attorney who can assist in directing the investigative procedure and thereby help to avoid any pitfalls that might later prove detrimental to the case.

Before commencing the investigation, ask for exemplars written by any potential suspects. Since many anonymous communications are sent by the "victim" to himself, ask for exemplars from the recipient, explaining that this is standard procedure in this type of investigation.* Requesting that the victim recall in detail all circumstances surrounding the receipt of the anonymous writing and whether anyone close to him or her might be the possible perpetrator are also important steps in the investigation.

To avoid possible legal difficulties, do not single out any one particular suspect when seeking known writing samples, but include exemplars from several possible suspects. When asking for writing samples, remember that like must be compared to like: handwriting to handwriting, printing to printing, graffiti to graffiti, initials to initials.

At all costs, premature opinions and/or accusations are to be avoided. No opinion, either verbal or written, should be rendered until all evidence has been thoroughly considered. In most anonymous writing cases there is more than meets the eye. A hasty response may be erroneous and could result in ruined friendship, ridicule, remorse or a potential lawsuit for slander.

If the anonymous writer's first communication does not give the desired effect, it will often be followed by additional notes or letters. Unless the first letter is especially threatening, advise the victim to wait for the next correspondence, which is apt to result in additional clues helpful in identifying the writer. Typically, the writer of multiple anonymous letters will be unable to recall the many details he or she uti-

*Request exemplars normally require special consideration. The writer may make attempts at disguising the request writing, especially if he or she is also the author of the anonymous writing. Extensive exemplars may be necessary, and the examiner will possibly require standards that are written with the non-dominant hand. (See Chapter 8 for additional information regarding standard procedures for requesting exemplars.)

lized in writing or transmitting the first letter. Writing habits are likely to show through more readily in subsequent letters, and any consistencies between the first letter and those which follow may in fact lead to identification.

Reading the letter aloud several times will help clarify its content and meaning. When multiple communications are involved, considering each in chronological order will sometimes reveal the writer's identity and/or motive.

All evidence, including envelopes and any inserted material, should be photographed and preserved in sheet protectors. All materials must be handled carefully to avoid damage and to minimize the possibility of obliterating fingerprints and/or other evidence. Also important in criminal cases is maintaining the chain of custody by keeping a record of the document's possession, verifying to whom the document was delivered, on what date, details regarding the condition of the document, and information about the return of the document. This assists in preserving documents in their original condition and deters evidence tampering.

Frequently the anonymous writer is careless in addressing the envelope, inadvertently leaving clues to his identity. Unfortunately, in some cases the recipient carelessly discards the envelope, not realizing its importance to the investigation of the case. The overall writing style or the manner in which the numbers and punctuation are written on the envelope may be less disguised than the letter itself. Other clues, such as the alignment of the writing and its arrangement on the envelope, may also prove beneficial. Examine the postmark for date, time, and zip code, although the smart criminal will mail the letter away from his home or work place. Consider whether the envelope is at all unusual in such features as size or color. (Baker says that women are more inclined to utilize distinctive materials than are men.)

Scrutinize the envelope flap for trace evidence such as lipstick, or hair which may help lead to a solution in the case.

Is the paper common or unusual? If uncommon, where can the paper be obtained and does the victim know anyone who uses such paper? If a watermark is present, it might be an additional clue in identifying the paper source and perhaps connecting it to the writer. If the note or letter is photocopied or printed, as in instances when the same correspondence is distributed to two or more people, there may be markings and other evidence useful in leading to identification of the photocopier or printer.

Although many types of pens are readily obtained, the kind used may lend more clues to the writer's identity. Today, ball-point pens are probably worthless as a factor in identification due to their prevalence. Fountain pens, however, may be more valuable in that they are now relatively uncommon. They are sometimes favored by people who are artistic or who appreciate the arts, and seem to be gaining in popularity with business executives.

Careful investigation may yield pointers as to nationality, age, gender, and social or educational status. Clues to the writer's age or educational level will show up in grammatical expressions, the words chosen, and the manner in which sentences are constructed. The general rule is that a person cannot rise above his natural skill level. He may utilize worse handwriting, poorer spelling and punctuation, or cruder language than normal, but the pretense is likely to be penetrated if he attempts to appear more educated or socially refined than he is. A well-written letter will automatically eliminate any suspect who is uneducated or semi-literate.

Does the writer use multi-syllabic words and are they used properly? Have they been spelled correctly? Are sentences complete? Does sentence structure correspond with the apparent educational level of the writing? Are thoughts continuous? If multiple letters are under investigation, are there repeated words or phrases that will tie the letters to one author and help to identify the writer? Does the grammatical style and/or use of idioms suggest the person's ethnic background or tie him to a particular part of the country? This can be especially helpful in racially diverse locales such as Hawaii.

Disguise in Anonymous Writing Cases

Disguise is an attempt on the part of the author to alter the appearance and features of the writing in order to avoid detection. This usually involves changing the pictorial quality of the writing or printing by creating an awkward or labored product designed to conceal one's normal writing idiosyncrasies.

Such attempts may fool the untrained eye, and the writer may be quite successful in disguising a signature or only a few words. But in lengthy communications he or she generally slips back into natural writing habits so that the disguise eventually wears thin. The writer who wishes to mimic someone else's writing and conceal his own natural habits at the same time faces an extremely difficult task which is likely to fail. Likewise, in a series of anonymous letters the perpetrator is apt to forget the details of his disguise from one letter to the next, offering the investigator more clues to his identity.

One author of a series of anonymous hate notes left in a fellow-employee's locker foolishly made little effort to avoid detection, even of some obvious features like capital letters. In comparing the notes with the writing of the perpetrator, the source of the anonymous material becomes readily apparent. (See Figure 11.1.)

Attempts at disguise usually include the alteration of obvious handwriting features such as size and capital letter formations, or the overall style might be changed. A common form of disguise is to alter the slant of one's handwriting, either from forward to vertical or vice-versa. Maintaining such a disguise is rather difficult and the person will sometimes inadvertently use his natural slant for isolated words. As David Ellen suggests, "lapses of concentration cause reversion to the natural method."[6]

Altering little except the slant of the writing on a falsified hotel guest complaint was the fatal mistake of one jealous individual who wanted to get a co-worker fired. Transparencies of individual letters from the guest complaint were repositioned over the suspect's known writing, shifting them so that the slant of one coincided with the slant of the other. The writer was easily identified by individual letters and in some cases entire words that closely matched his own. (See Figure 11.2.)

Malformations or gross distortions such as false tremor or exaggerated letters are also rather common forms of disguise. The perpetrator may choose to write with the non-dominant hand, use a different pen hold, or an unusual type of pen—a thick-nibbed pen such as a felt tip marker, for example. Irregular pen pressure or smudging may also be employed in an attempt to mislead.

---

6. David Ellen, *Scientific Examination of Documents*, Chichester, England: Ellis Horwood Limited, 1993.

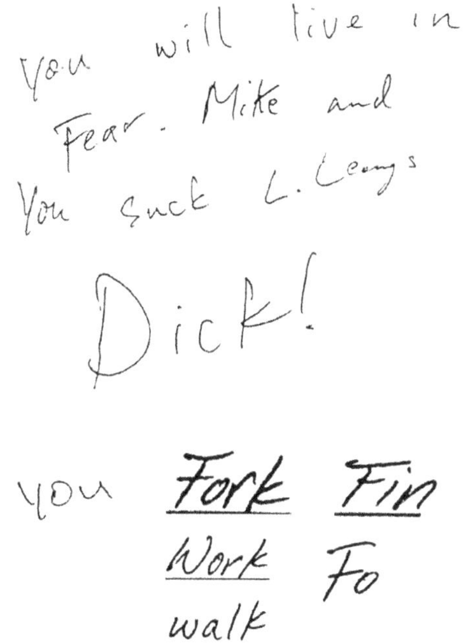

Fig. 11.1—Identification of anonymous writer due to little attempt at disguise. Note similar letter forms (*y, F, k*) in anonymous writing (top) compared to known writing (bottom).

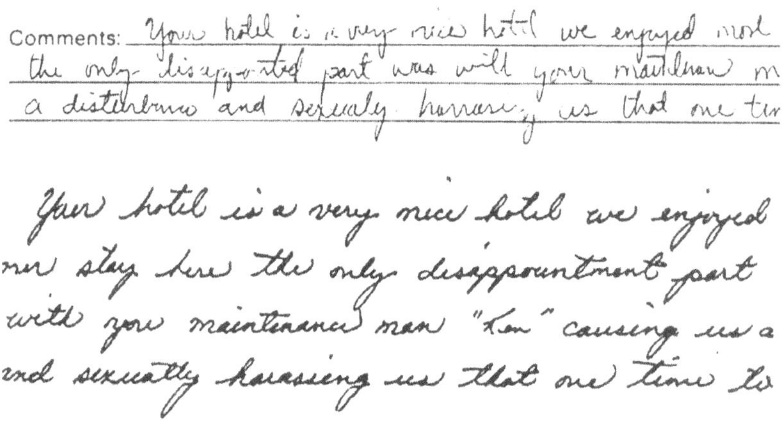

Fig. 11.2—Attempt at disguise by change of slant. Note numerous similarities between anonymous writing (top) and request writing (bottom).

Printing is a frequent method of disguise in anonymous notes. However, although perhaps more easily controlled than handwriting due to each letter being written separately, printing has as much potential for uniqueness as handwriting. If the writer is unfamiliar with printing, he may use a combination of printing and writing, in which case the written characters will probably match those of his genuine handwriting.

Collecting standards of comparison may be more burdensome when the anonymous note or letter is printed. Sources for known printing might include check registers, envelopes, applications, forms, personal telephone directories, ledgers or notebooks.

Assumed illiteracy is often utilized as a red herring. Many anonymous writers are educated and they sometimes attempt to depreciate their script to make it look as though it is from an ignorant person. Hanna Sulner writes that "deliberately misspelled words and other errors in many cases point immediately to an educated person simulating illiterate writing."[7]

Consider that careful arrangement, good paragraph habits and precise punctuation are not normally signs of an illiterate or semiliterate person. Certain letter formations such as fluid strokes, figure eight structures or Greek es will sometimes belie the writer's real skill. On the other hand, a poorly educated person is apt to have a consistently clumsy writing style with awkward formations and poor marginal or paragraph habits.

Penetrating the Disguise

In anonymous writing cases the ultimate objective is normally to identify the author. Some anonymous writers are adept enough that their disguise is impenetrable, but most will be unable to conceal their identities from the astute examiner.

Baker recommends that in determining whether a handwriting is disguised, two important factors be considered: 1) It is impossible for a person to write better than his natural best hand and 2) a person writing in a disguised manner cannot write as well as in his natural hand.[8]

Any writing exhibiting rhythm, speed, fluency, smoothness and uniformity suggests an experienced writer with an adeptness at setting words to paper. Such writing automatically becomes a standard for comparison for the purpose of eliminating any writer whose skills do not measure up to these qualities.

---

7. Hanna F. Sulner, *Disputed Documents*, Dobbs Ferry, New York: Oceana Publications, 1966.

8. Baker, *ibid.*, p.289.

Attempts at disguise generally alter only the pictorial effect of the handwriting and not the writer's idiosyncrasies. Unique habits of writing certain letters will be difficult for the writer to eliminate.

To prove that two handwritings were produced by the same person, sufficient similarities which cannot be accidental must be shown to exist in each. To conclude that two handwritings were produced by different writers, ample discrepancies that cannot be accounted for by accident or disguise must be found between the two.

Care must be taken by the handwriting examiner that an identification not be based on one or two similarities between the anonymous writing and a suspect's standards, even if the feature appears to be unique. The evidence must be cumulative, with numerous similarities lending weight to the conclusion. A case involving a handprinted note placed on the windshield of an employee's car serves to illustrate this point. In their eagerness to find the culprit, the company's management team pulled personnel records of several potential suspects. An unusual printed g on the note appeared to coincide with a similar g found on the application of one of the recipient's co-workers. Fortunately, the company requested my services to investigate the anonymous note and to confirm their suspicions. While the unique g formation did appear in the writing of their suspect, there were few additional structures that matched. In fact, the same type of g was used by four out of the twelve people investigated, including the victim herself.

A common fallacy in dealing with documentary evidence is to take each coincidence separately and to show that a similar coincidence exists or does not exist in some other writer. This would be logical reasoning if any one coincidence so considered could in itself be conclusive, but it does not meet the requirements of competent document examination. The evidence must be cumulative; the weight or proof of the evidence must depend not on any one single coincidence, but on numerous coincidences. While each by itself would be inconclusive, all taken together may lead to an identification.

Comparison Features

The investigator should examine literally every handwriting or printing feature of the anonymous letter and compare each of them to the exemplars provided. The examiner may choose to utilize a worksheet such as those presented in this book to record similarities and differences.

The following characteristics are to be considered:

- Size—absolute size and size of midzone, upper zone and lower zone formations
- Proportions of letters, upper loops and lower loops
- Letter connections—angles, arcades, garlands, or threads
- Punctuation style and placement. (Over-punctuation may be a clue.)
- Style and placement of diacritic marks
- Spacing—letter, word and line
- Margin habits
- Individual letter formations
- Numbers. Columns of figures written in one sitting tend to develop a particular slope, while those written at intervals are usually perpendicular. It is not likely that these features would be successfully disguised. Numbers are often not disguised, especially on envelopes containing anonymous material.
- Unusual grammatical or spelling errors
- Habitual word arrangement or sentence construction
- i dots and periods. The method of dotting the i and making periods may be significant as the writer is probably unaware of any individuality in making these small marks. Some writers habitually place the dot far to the right or left, very high, exceptionally low, or as a continuation of the degree of slant. Some writers do not make normal round dots, but instead use dashes, blobs or circles.

12. Disguised Writing

Disguised writing results from an attempt to conceal one's identity by modifying the manner or appearance of his or her handwriting or signature. The person intends to conceal recognition by way of one or more deliberate departures from normal writing habits.

Disguise may be utilized any time the writer does not wish to be identified. The person may not want to be exposed for having written anonymous notes, for example. Or there might be a deliberate disguise of one's signature with the intent of denying it later on.

Sometimes there are attempts at mimicking another person's writing in which case the disguise is made even more difficult, as normal writing habits must be covered and foreign ones simultaneously adopted. Such scenarios make the document examiner's job even more challenging.

When investigating what appears to be disguised writing, it is easy for even seasoned handwriting examiners to make honest mistakes due to the complexity involved in the disguise process. With experience, competent examiners learn to discern whether the differences between two writings are due to natural variation, disguise or different writers.

Not all disguised writing can be identified. With skill and practice, it may be possible to adopt enough disguise to fool even the experts, particularly when short passages of text are involved. But unless the perpetrator has special skills, including an in-depth knowledge of handwriting, usually the disguise breaks down after a few words or, in more successful attempts, possibly a few lines of writing.

Most attempts at disguise are unimaginative and relatively simple. Usually the writer chooses a method of alteration that will affect the pictorial look of the writing—that which strikes the eye at first glance. The pictorial aspects of the writing are almost entirely a function of a few features including size, slant, capital letters and degree of embellishment, along with some obvious features of letter design, most of which are relatively easy to alter.

Whatever method is chosen, few writers can disguise their writing so that it is not ultimately recognizable.

The primary reason that writing is difficult to disguise is that it is so closely tied to one's memory for and habitual execution of letter shapes, as well as an individual's nervous system and physical makeup. It is extremely difficult to concentrate on altering all of the features that make up one's writing, except for perhaps a very short period of time. Changing an obvious writing feature like the capital letters is somewhat easy, because there are breaks in the writing before and after each capital, giving the person time to think about the movements of each letter. But when attempting more complicated changes—the forms of lower case letters, for example—the writer will have trouble remembering the intended changes each time the letter occurs while maintaining the rhythm, fluency and naturalness of the writing at the same time.

The person most likely to succeed at disguise has at least some artistic ability, is educated in various disciplines of handwriting, handles or studies numerous signatures, and/or has mastered several writing systems or styles. Successful disguise also depends on the person's manual skills and imagination.

Generally, the person attempting disguise will change those writing features that are most striking to the eye, such as slant, size, capital letters and loops, the obvious features that give writing its pictorial quality. But the attempt usually fails when it comes to obscuring the minute, inconspicuous features of the writing, even when the person is aware of them.

With some exceptions, an individual's natural, non-disguised handwriting displays an internal consistency characterized by similarity in letter forms, shape, sizes, arrangement and proportion. This gives most natural writing a certain flow or overall organization. The rhythm of one's writing is best when the script is spontaneous and there is little or no thought given to the details of the construction of the writing.

Disguise calls for focus and concentration, not so much on what is being written, but how. Such intense focus results in variable slant and/or awkward movements, connections and letter forms. Disguised writing usually lacks internal consistency and nearly always contains conflicting writing habits because there is a battle between natural writing habits and attempts to suppress them. Disparity within disguised writing is apt to be especially noticeable in lengthy passages of text, which will often appear disjointed or non-rhythmic. However, on a cautionary note, handwriting can have an awkward, arrhythmic appearance without any intent to disguise. Some people naturally have widely variable writing and that possibility should be closely considered. Also, it is possible for non-disguised writing to seem awkward or unusual due to the effect of a number of internal or external factors as considered elsewhere in this book.

When the person's attention relaxes or his mind wanders, habitual writing habits tend to creep in so that portions of the writing will remain undisguised. This is especially so with extended writing. When disguise is suspected, an effective process is to start the examination toward the end of the writing, working one's way toward the beginning, as it is likely that the disguise will wear thin as the writer proceeds.

With anonymous note cases consisting of multiple communications, sometimes the perpetrator forgets the type of disguise or the details of individual formations used in the earlier letters. In such cases the person often fails to utilize disguise on the envelope as well and may also overlook the construction of numbers. (See Chapter 11.)

Following are some general considerations regarding disguise:

- Attempts at disguise are rarely original and usually entail some simple attempt at hiding one's identity.
- Gross alteration in slant is one of the most common attempts at disguise.
- Writing that looks disguised may not be disguised at all. Some people naturally have non-rhythmic, inconsistent writing, which highlights the need for sufficient exemplars.
- Not all disguised writing can be identified or attributed to a specific suspect.
- Any deliberate change of obvious writing features (e.g., slant, size, capital letters) will have a profound effect on the writing's overall appearance.
- Disguised writing is seldom consistent, especially in lengthy passages.
- The greater the concentration on the disguise attempt, the more the writing will depart from natural fluency and rhythm. The internal consistency of writing will be disrupted, causing an awkward or unnatural look.
- In an extended passage of writing the disguise usually weakens toward the end, either due to the writer becoming tired or losing concentration. The final paragraphs of a disguised writing will

bear more of a resemblance to the person's normal writing than what's been written before.

- Handwriting on envelopes is often not as thoroughly disguised as the contents.
- Request writings are subject to disguise, particularly if the suspect is guilty of authoring the writing in question.
- When attempting disguise, writers tend to make difficult letters larger to compensate for lack of skill.
- Zonal proportions are rarely modified in disguised writing.
- Block lettering is seldom disguised as people erroneously believe block formations alone to be impenetrable.

Types of Disguise

Disguise is rarely original and usually consists of superficial changes that affect the overall appearance of the writing but not the details. The average person is mistaken in believing this is the only requirement to render their writing unidentifiable.

In attempting disguise, the person may choose to alter any of the following features of the writing:

Slant—Altering the slant of one's writing produces essentially a pictorial change. Generally this entails a pronounced switch from right slant to vertical or left, or from backhand to forward slant. Altering the slant has a general effect on the letter forms and the overall fluency of the writing. It frequently causes the line of writing to ascend (in the case of assuming vertical or backhand) or descend (when adopting a more forward slope). Often the person's usual slant will find its way back into the disguised writing. However, not all variable slant is indicative of disguise, since there are some people whose writing slant changes naturally within one passage of text or from one writing session to another. It is also to be noted that people sometimes change the slant of their writing slightly when writing at different speeds or in different positions, so this feature should be evaluated carefully. Reaching conclusions about disguise based on slant change or variability may require numerous exemplars written over a period of time and under different circumstances.

Capital letters—Altering these obvious features affects the pictorial quality of the writing. As with a change of slant, to the novice this may seem an adequate disguise. It is relatively easy to maintain the disguise of capital letters, considering that writing pauses occur both before and usually after them, which gives the person added time to think. When the capital letters are the primary difference between two writings (especially signatures) they should be ignored and conclusions based primarily on comparison of other features.

Size—To a certain extent, changing writing size alters the overall look of the script. Usually this entails writing larger than normal and, like changing capital letters, is a relatively easy type of disguise to maintain. In most cases when there is a deliberate change in writing size the proportional relationship between letters and parts of letters will remain consistent and undisguised. It is especially difficult to disguise the ratios of both upper and lower extenders simultaneously.

Exchanging allographs—This method of disguise involves the substitution of cursive for printing and vice-versa. A change from script to printing usually eliminates any connecting strokes between letters, which are valuable identification features. This method can be effective, depending on the type of comparison standards available for the examination.

Substitution of lower case letter forms—Changing individual letter forms is the most difficult disguise to maintain. It requires considerable practice and concentration, often at the expense of natural flow and rhythm. It is most common to change the first and/or last letters of words which will cause the most immediately noticeable effect.

Use of non-dominant hand—This is a somewhat uncommon disguise technique which grossly changes the pictorial quality of the writing and almost always leaves it with a clumsy, awkward appearance. It usually involves a change in slant. However, the examiner must be aware that ambidextrous people are capable of writing fluently with either hand. Also, some people can produce mirror writing, sometimes at the same time the other hand is writing normally. Questions about handedness should be asked and adequate comparison standards must be collected for the examination.

Change of writing instrument—This method can produce differences in pressure, shading, line width and strength of individual strokes. Felt-tip pen writing may successfully mask the minor features of writing due to the thickness of the pen and the black trail of ink that it produces. However, a mere change in pen will not likely affect important identifying features like arrangement and letter proportion.

Arrangement patterns—The writer may think to alter the way his or her writing normally appears on the page, the usual margin habits, spacing between lines, or paragraph indentations. Less likely to be considered are word and letter spacing, valuable to the identification process. Often arrangement patterns on envelopes remain undisguised.

Writing speed—A drastic alteration in speed (fast to slow or slow to fast) will affect the writing's overall appearance. The slower the writing, the more thick, heavy or labored it is apt to appear. A fast writing or signature might be "scrawled" so that individual letters cannot be distinguished and identified.

Introduction of irregularities—An educated person might try to write as an illiterate, either in handwriting style or grammar, or an adult may write in a childish, uneducated fashion. This is sometimes discovered by the occasional fluid or sophisticated letter which belies mature writing and education. Deliberate misspellings will possibly be introduced as well, and may be accompanied by words that only a more educated person would likely know.

Use of tremor—Shaky or wavering writing may be utilized to feign illness or old age, or possibly to distort the writing so that minor features are less apparent. Areas of smoothness where the person forgot to write in a tremulous manner point toward disguise and, if sufficient, may assist in identification.

Variation of initial or terminal strokes—Adding, omitting or varying initial or terminal strokes may alter the writing superficially, but will have little effect on the writing as a whole. As the passage of writing proceeds, the person may relapse into using habitual initial or final strokes. People are generally most conscious of the first part of letters, words and lines, so finals are more important overall when trying to penetrate disguise.

Use of circle dots—This also affects the writing minimally as dots and periods have little to do with the overall structure of the writing. Forgetting to disguise the placement of such features, however, may prove significant.

Often forgotten in the disguise attempt are writing arrangement, numbers, spacing (words, letters, lines), formation and relative placement of punctuation and diacritics, titles such as *Mr., Mrs., Ms.* or *Dr.*, and embellishments including flourishes, ornamentations and underlinings.

Self-disguised Signatures

Signatures are sometimes altered in an effort to render them unrecognizable, usually so that the individual can later deny that he or she signed some document. For example, a person writes a check on his own account, but deliberately alters the writing and signature on the check so that later he can claim the checkbook was stolen and an unknown perpetrator then wrote and signed the check in question. Or, a signature is deliberately altered on a contractual agreement with the intent of reneging on the obligation at some later date.

Typical comments of a person denying his own altered signature are "I never write my *J* like that" or "I never make a long final at the end of my name, so it can't be my signature."

Usually when self-disguise is employed much of the signature remains unaffected. As disguise is generally unimaginative, the obvious features of the signature are likely to be changed, but its details will remain intact. In most cases relatively good fluidity and fine details are retained, but there will be some obvious discrepancies as in slant or capital letter formation, features that affect primarily the pictorial look of the signature.

This is unlike typical simulated signatures where the more obvious features are likely to be correct in construction, but the inconspicuous details are incorrect and the signature lacks fluidity of movement.

One method of self-disguise is to create a completely different signature design, so that the end product looks nothing at all like the person's usual signature. Obviously, the purpose here is to throw off anyone who will later see the signature and immediately assume it is invalid because it "doesn't match." In these cases successful identification may not be possible due to the extent of the grossly altered signature formations.

With respect to most disguised writing, numerous exemplars will be required if the examiner is to reach solid conclusions. Writer identification or elimination will depend on the skill of the person perpetrating the disguise, the amount of writing in question, the sufficiency and appropriateness of comparison material and the expertise of the handwriting examiner.

Determining the likely method of disguise will assist in knowing the types of standards to collect for the comparison process. If it appears that the writing was disguised by a change of slant, the examiner may need to request writing using a different slant. If the person changed various letter styles, a number of normal course of business samples—written at different times and for different purposes—will probably suffice.

The following tips are recommended for evaluating writing suspected of disguise:

- Start the examination at the end of a passage of writing where the person is more likely to fall back into normal writing habits.
- Ignore the overall appearance of the writing and focus on the inconspicuous features.
- Place less emphasis on letter design and more emphasis on less apparent writing features such as spacing, margins, proportions, pressure, punctuation, baselines, letter connections and i dots.
- Watch for areas of inconsistency where the writer reverts back to his normal style.
- Evaluate any idiosyncrasies in the disguised writing to see if they match the suspect's writing.
- Focus more attention on the endings of letters, words and paragraphs than on capital letters and initial formations.
- Unnecessarily corrected letters are suspect for disguise, especially capital letters.
- When breaks occur in a person's normal signature, those breaks will usually also appear in the disguised signature.
- Size ratios of individual names generally remain consistent in disguised signatures when compared to the person's known signatures.

13. Special Considerations

A number of physical stress factors may significantly alter an individual's writing—injuries or deformities to the writing hand and arm, diseases and afflictions of the central nervous system, or problems with the muscles and joints of the writing hand, for instance.

Writing can also be affected by alcohol or infirmities related to the aging process. When any of these considerations surround the production of writing or signatures, it may be necessary for the examiner to investigate further.

Influence of Alcohol

Is it possible to make an identification when comparing a person's alcohol-affected writing with his or her normal writing? This question arises in cases in which defendants claim they did not sign some document, often a consent to search form, after being arrested for driving "under the influence."

To answer this question, we must consider alcohol's effects in general and on handwriting in particular.

Alcohol produces known effects on the chemistry and physiology of the body which result in functional problems. It has adverse influences on handwriting which understandably vary with the amount of alcohol consumed, the writer's blood alcohol level and general physical condition, and his or her tolerance for alcohol. The situation becomes more complicated if the inebriated person has also consumed other drugs or is suffering from any illness.

Essentially, alcohol is a central nervous system depressant. It exerts its primary effects on the lower levels of the brain where the activity of the thalamic structures and limbic system are the first to become depressed. This slowing of the brain spreads as intoxication increases.[1]

As a person becomes progressively intoxicated, motor coordination suffers and concentration and balance diminish. At the same time, the intoxicated person's handwriting normally maintains forward momentum.[2] Consequently, intricate writing movements cannot be ac-

1. R. R. Julien, *A Primer of Drug Action, 3rd. Ed.*, San Francisco: W. H. Freeman and Co., 1981.
2. Ordway Hilton, "A Study of the Influence of Alcohol on Handwriting," Journal of Forensic Science, Vol. 14, 1969, pp. 309-316.

complished as effectively as when sober, yet the writing moves rapidly forward. The result is usually larger writing than normal that is more spread out and less precise.

The intoxicated person does not normally lose grip strength,[3] suggesting that the writing is not apt to become appreciably tremulous or weakened. It has also been shown that automated tasks are relatively easy for the person under the influence of alcohol, an indication that the signature, being strongly habituated, may be produced with relative accuracy. However, as eye-tracking diminishes with alcohol consumption[4] the writer may have trouble following a straight baseline so that the signature will possibly droop toward the end.

It is common knowledge that when an alcoholic is sober, he or she often has "the shakes" which would of course reflect as tremor in the handwriting. So, while a few cocktails will impair the writing of non-alcoholics, they will markedly improve the writing of the alcohol-dependent.

Andrew Bradley's Training Course in Forensic Document Examination describes some of the most obvious influences on writing produced "under the influence," including:

- lack of coordination causing poor letter form
- enlarged size
- irregular spacing and lateral expansion
- uneven baseline
- illegibility
- misplaced and ill-formed t crosses and i dots
- missing letters or parts of letters
- pressure variation

Studies conducted by Bradley and others indicate that although there are observable signs of alcohol's impact on handwriting, the effects vary considerably from person to person. As one might expect, an increase in blood alcohol level causes the writing of most people to become increasingly distorted, larger and less evenly aligned. There will also likely be difficulty writing sharp angles. However, these indicators do not hold true in every case, and no standard pattern of deterioration in the

3. D. E. Hartman, *Neuropsychological Toxicology: Identification and Assessment of Human Neurotoxic Syndromes*, New York: Pergamon Press, 1988.

4. Hartman, *ibid.*

writing of alcoholics has been documented.

When intoxication at the time of writing is a possibility, the ideal situation would be to have exemplary material written under the same circumstances, but that is usually difficult if not impossible. Nevertheless, it appears that in most cases there is a sufficient number of similarities between one's handwriting produced under the influence of alcohol and his or her normal writings to make a positive identification. This is particularly true with regard to signatures which are more or less automatic.

Fig. 13.1—Signature "under the influence" (top) versus non-intoxicated signature (bottom)

Considering the foregoing, it is often possible to identify a writer based on normal writing compared to alcohol-induced writing. Consider Figure 13.1 where the signature written under the influence of alcohol is notably similar to the writer's normal signature, with the primary difference being in the lateral expansion.

Handwriting of the Elderly

Signatures of elderly persons are frequently at issue in cases regarding matters of probate, including wills, codicils to wills or transfer of property. Unfortunately these people are often victims of greedy family members who try to manipulate distribution of their estates for purely personal gain. Sometimes the perpetrators of these acts resort to outright forgery and at other times they trick the person into believing they're signing something beneficial when in fact the signature ends up on a document that is ultimately harmful to the victim.

Due to the natural aging process, one's writing changes over time, often deteriorating in later years as muscles and joints stiffen and physical senses diminish. Changes usually affect the elderly writer's skill level, legibility, smoothness of execution and letter design. Often the elderly person writes more slowly, uncertainly or erratically, with weakened pen grip. There may be tremor, poor spacing and alignment, irregular formations and unusual or distorted letter forms.

The degree of writing deterioration depends on individual circumstances including type and severity of illnesses, medications, mental state and degeneration of nerves and muscles. Usually the deterioration of writing is gradual, although changes can take place rapidly as in the case of sudden illness. Those elderly people of sound mind and body will likely have relatively normal writing, while others will write with poor coordination and exceptional tremor. There is of course no way to determine with any degree of certainty the chronological age of the writer.

The quality of the elderly person's writing may fluctuate as his or her condition improves and deteriorates, or as medications take effect and wear off. It is therefore especially important to obtain contemporaneous exemplars if at all possible when their signatures are in question. It may also be helpful to know the types of illnesses and medications and their likely effects on the writing. This consideration becomes further complicated when the person suffers from multiple illnesses or is taking a number of medications simultaneously.

It is important to consider the alleged circumstances surrounding signatures of the elderly, including the person's physical and mental state at the time and any unusual writing positions such as lying in bed.

The key to successfully working cases involving signatures of the elderly is determining the difference between those characteristics that result from age or illness and those that are attributable to forgery. Even though elderly writing might be tremulous, misaligned or uncertain, there is still apt to be an internal consistency in the signatures which will likely not be present in simulations. Generally, the forger who simulates an elderly person's writing focuses on the pictorial appearance of the writing, including tremor and awkwardness of letters.

When investigating these signatures the actual letter forms are not as significant as the movements that make up the letters. The elderly person has habitual writing movements that have developed over a lifetime and these patterns are not likely to change appreciably in one instance. Therefore, if any movement in a questioned signature is incorrect when compared to the known, the signature is probably not genuine.

The forger may make the signature tremulous even when the known writing is not, thinking the tremor will be attributed to advanced age rather than imitation. Simulated tremor is rarely consistent. It is often overly tremulous or shaky in the wrong places (in downstrokes instead of upstrokes, for example). In many cases portions of the signature in question will be written smoothly when the victim is actually incapable of writing such even strokes. Sometimes pen lifts caused by the forgery process can be identified as such because the elderly person does not have the ability to replace the writing instrument to the paper as carefully as in the simulation.

Elderly people often have difficulty maintaining full grip on the writing instrument, especially when executing upstrokes. Their writing will therefore sometimes be weaker in the upward movements of upper zone letters, some of which may take on an angular shape as pen grip is readjusted. The forger, on the other hand, usually has a tight grip on the pen, resulting in heavier than normal writing pressure.

Misalignment in elderly people's signatures may be the result of poor eyesight or lack of muscular control. In some instances unusual writing position will also come into play. Oftentimes there will be different alignment for the first name and the last, perhaps because the writer paused in between or shifted positioning of the writing hand. Forgers tend to overlook the importance of alignment and will often write on a more consistent baseline than that of the person's usual signature.

Considerations listed in the chart below may be helpful in examining cases involving the writing of elderly people.

Alzheimer's Disease

The handwriting of the elderly becomes more complex when Alzheimer's disease is involved.

Alzheimer's is a common form of dementia affecting approximately seven percent of those over 65 in the United States. However, it can afflict people under the age of 50 as well. As yet there is no prevention or cure for Alzheimer's, nor is there any certainty as to its cause, although there is indication that it is hereditary.

In most cases the disease begins with subtle forgetfulness, but as it progresses it results in more definite lapses of memory, odd behavior and difficulty functioning normally. It is frequently characterized by disorientation, fluctuation of emotion and inability to recognize people. Usually the patient becomes disinterested in personal appearance and hygiene as well.

Genuine	Simulated
Poor form*	More consistent form
Poor quality*	Some smooth strokes, some not
Tremulous, but uniformly so	Tremor inconsistent, planned or exaggerated
Disrupted movement, but with internal consistency	Improper direction of stroke movement**
Abrupt changes in stroke direction	Slower, less impulsive changes in stroke direction
Pressure of up- and downstrokes maintained	Course, heavy pressure
Disrupted alignment	Difficulty maintaining same alignment
	Letter forms foreign to writer Elements beyond writer's ability
*If only one is affected, look for reasons other than age or illness. **Elderly person's are unlikely to alter lifelong movement habits.	

According to the Alzheimer's Disease Education and Referral Center, Alzheimer's is the most common form of dementia among older people. It involves the parts of the brain that control thought, memory and language. It may be characterized by aphasia (loss of ability to understand or express speech), alexia (inability to see or read words—"word blindness") and agraphia (inability to write).[5]

In the early stages of Alzheimer's there may be little change from the person's normal writing. However, as the disease progresses the patient's handwriting will display typical signs of aging, but to a marked degree. Increasing lack of fluency can be expected, along with inconsistent form, size and proportions, improper connections and extreme baseline variation. Omission of some letters and words, repetition of letters and illegible or meaningless writing are indicative of the patient's forgetfulness and confusion. In advanced stages of the disease the person may be entirely unable to write.

5. E. Edward Peeples & Hans-Leo Teulings, "The Brain and Handwriting," Seventh Biennial Conference of the International Graphonomics Society, London, Ontario, August 6-10, 1995.

In a study by Slavin, Phillips, et al. it was shown that irrespective of medication or severity, Alzheimer's patients produced writing strokes of significantly less consistent lengths than did the controls in the study. Additionally, unlike the controls, they frequently produced perseverations (repetitive movements as in too many arches for the letter n). The study suggests that Alzheimer's disease reflects a frontal rather than basal ganglia dysfunction which resembles that of Huntington's rather than Parkinson's disease patients.[6]

Examining the writing of Alzheimer's patients becomes doubly difficult due to any medications that have been prescribed to combat its symptoms. Numerous drugs have different effects on different patients and there may be gross fluctuations in the patient's writing, even over a short period of time. For example, tremor may be exhibited as a result of the disease and the patient may be prescribed medication to quell the tremor, after which the writing will appear less shaky. But at another time the patient may be given yet another drug that produces the side effect of even greater tremor than existed before.

While the handwriting examiner should not attempt to be an expert on the disease, it is nevertheless imperative to consider the possible effects of any medications that are prescribed. It will of course be important to obtain information about any drugs that were ingested prior to allegedly writing a questioned signature as well as the production of any exemplar signatures. Knowledge of the circumstances surrounding the signing may also prove useful to the examination.

---

6. M. J. Slavin, J. G. Phillips, J. L. Bradshaw, K. A. Hall, I. Presnell, "Consistency of Handwriting Movements in Dementia of the Alzheimer's Type," Journal of the International Neuropsychological Society, 1999 Jan; 5(1):20-5.

14. Case History No. 1

This case involves a dispute between BancUnion Trust, a Florida company, and David Murakami, a businessman from Hawaii.

Mr. Murakami is the president and CEO of Electronic Valet Systems, Inc., a leasing company. Over the years he has successfully conducted business with BancUnion Trust. BancUnion claims that Mr. Murakami has reneged on some business deals, one of which is the subject of this matter.

At issue are a number of signatures, although for the sake of simplicity only two of those in question are presented here. For ease of reference, the questioned signatures are referred to as Q1 and Q2.

Mr. Murakami claims that he did not sign his name to any of the disputed documents. He indicates that he once had a partner who involved his company in questionable business deals on more than one occasion, and claims that the business partner probably forged his signature on the documents in question.

Mr. Murakami's attorney produced several normal course of business documents bearing signatures known to have been written by Mr. Murakami close to the date of the signatures in question. A number of the known signatures are on other BancUnion documents, reflective of business transactions that are not in dispute. Six of the 20 known signatures are reproduced here and are referred to as K1 through K6.

Did Mr. Murakami sign his name to the documents in question? This can be answered by following the procedure laid out in Chapter 9.

General observations: Despite the poor quality of the two questioned signatures which can be attributed to the copy process, it is nevertheless evident that both are of substandard line quality. They appear tremulous and uncertain in direction and they lack natural, fluid formations. The skill level of the writer is low and/or the signatures are poorly simulated. Frequent adjustments of the pen, blunt starts and finishes and a drawn look point toward slow writing movement. Their pictorial quality is vastly different from that of the known signatures.

Arrangement: Alignment of the signatures in question is inconsistent with that of the knowns. The known signatures tend to ride above the printed line, while the questioned signatures closely hug the line. Any variability in the baseline of the knowns is accomplished by smoothness of transition, while the questioned signatures evidence jerky readjustments between letters.

Size and Proportions: While the absolute size of the questioned signatures is close to that of the knowns, letter proportions are incorrect. Note, for example, improper capital letter sizes compared to lower case letters as well as improper size of loop in the capital *M* of Q2 and none in the *M* of Q1. Ratios of the various writing features can be calculated by using the techniques given in Chapter 4. This is likely to be more accurate than relying on writing size which may have been affected by the copy process.

Pressure: This feature is difficult to assess with absolute certainty due to poor copy quality of the questioned writing and absence of the original. However, it is evident that the pressure in the questioned signatures varies considerably, unlike the knowns which evidence more consistent shading.

Spacing: Spacing between names of the questioned signatures is generally wider than between names of the knowns. Letter spacing is erratic versus relatively consistent.

Connecting strokes: Connections between letters of the known signatures are primarily garland formations, smoothly executed. Those of the questioned signatures are uncertain and, in some cases, slightly angular due to momentary stops of the pen.

Hiatuses, pen lifts: Breaks in the writing line of Q1 appear in the *D*, between *D* and *a*, between *r* and *a* and between *a* and *m*. In Q2 there are probably breaks between *i* and *d*, in the capital *M* and between *r* and *k*, although there is uncertainty in this regard due to the poor quality of the questioned material. The individual names of each known signature are written continuously, without breaks.

Initial and terminal strokes: Blunt beginnings and endings are evident in the questioned signatures, while they are tapered in the knowns. The final stroke of Murakami in both questioned signatures is incorrect both in shape and movement.

Slant: The slant pattern of the questioned signatures is variable and apparently disrupted, unlike the more consistent slant pattern evidenced in the knowns. Note especially the slant of the capitals and the letters that immediately follow.

Questioned

Q1:

Q2:

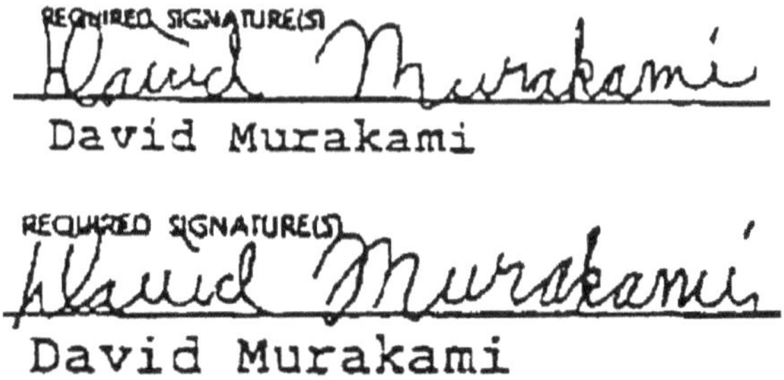

Fig. 14.1—Questioned signatures

Known

K1:

K2:

K3:

K4:

K5:

K6:

Fig. 14.2—Known signatures

Punctuation and diacritics: The i dots of the name David in the questioned signatures are heavy, deliberate and placed low, unlike those in the standards. The *i* dots at the end of the questioned signatures are also heavy and are not an extension of the final stroke of the signature as in the knowns.

Individual letters: Most of the letters of the questioned signatures are misshapen and poorly written. Note especially the capitals, the *d* in *David* and the *r, k* and *m* of *Murakami.*

Conclusion: The questioned signatures are vastly different from the standards in nearly every respect. They do not match pictorially and are of substandard movement and line quality which is evident despite being suboptimal copies. They are incorrect proportionally and in alignment, spacing and slant. Connections are poorly executed and movements are incorrect, as are most of the individual letters. There is overwhelming evidence that Mr. Murakami did not sign the questioned documents.

Epilogue: Mr. Murakami's attorney forwarded to BancUnion the handwriting examination report stating the opinion that he did not sign his name to the documents in question. Neither Mr. Murakami nor his attorney have heard from BancUnion since then, so it is assumed that they have dropped the matter. As a substantial amount of money was involved, it is likely that BancUnion hired their own handwriting examiner who agreed, otherwise a battle of the experts would have ensued.

As an aside, Mr. Murakami's former business partner has since been imprisoned for unrelated criminal activity.

15. Case History No. 2

In 2001 a suspicious postcard was received via U.S. Mail by the Sheraton Waikiki Hotel. The postcard, addressed to the hotel's personnel and employment manager, was signed "Mrs. Watanabe." The writer claimed to be an employee of Japan Airlines and stated she had been a guest at the hotel where she was allegedly intimidated and sexually harassed by one of the security guards.

The named security guard, who heretofore had been an outstanding employee, was shocked when confronted with the allegation and claimed that he did not recall any interactions with a female with the name Watanabe. His security log for the day of the alleged incident was reviewed, but failed to reveal anything incriminating.

Around the same time period various employees of the hotel began receiving anonymous letters and faxes that were either handwritten, computer generated, or both. Due to a number of other odd goings-on at the hotel, the personnel manager and director of security began to suspect one of their employees as the sender of the anonymous postcard and other material.

Armed with the questioned postcard, faxes and letters along with numerous handwriting samples of the suspected employee, the security manager sought an evaluation of the writing in hopes of identifying the perpetrator.

The suspect's handwriting exemplars were extensive and therefore only one page of them is reproduced here for comparison purposes.

General observations: The questioned writing is of poor line quality. Low skill level is initially suspected, however there are periodic letter formations that are more smoothly constructed, so it is possible that the apparent skill level may be due to disguise. Note the formation of numerals that comprise the zip code, suggesting more fluidity and skill than initially strikes the eye. One would not suspect a Japan Airlines employee to write so clumsily, but this would of course have to be investigated further. The speed of the writing is very slow and deliberate overall, with a few instances of more rapid movements. As with the skill level, the slowness of the writing might be attributable to disguise.

Arrangement: The postcard writing is arranged somewhat haphazardly with variable paragraph construction, shifting alignment and uncertain margins. This is also true of the suspect's known writing, especially those samples written on un-ruled paper which are not shown here. Lines that droop downward toward the end are present in known samples as well as in the postcard writing.

Fig. 15.1—Questioned postcard

Size and Proportions: In the questioned writing both upper and lower zone extenders are approximately two to two and one-half the height of midzone letters. In both, numerals are large in comparison to lower case letters. In both, the upper portion of lower case *f* is short while the lower loop is enlarged.

Pressure: Pressure of the questioned writing is variable, with occasionally stronger pressure on downstrokes and at the completion of certain letters. The known writing is slightly heavier overall, with stronger pressure on downstrokes and at the completion of certain letters.

Spacing: Letter spacing is moderate to wide but variable in both the questioned and known. Word spacing is wide to extra wide and variable in both the questioned and known.

Connecting strokes: In the postcard writing connections are largely arcade formations. The known writing, having been written in more of a printed style, evidences a variety of connections, some of them arcades. Positive matches are shown in *o-n* connectors.

Initial and terminal strokes: Many initial strokes are similar in both writings, as shown in the comparison charts. Terminal strokes are strikingly similar in their forward, downward movements often made with added pressure (see comparison charts).

Slant: Rightward and variable in both questioned and known.

Punctuation: Periods are jabbed and placed at a far distance from preceding letters in both questioned and known.

Numerals: Although not included in the comparison charts, several similarities in form and placement were evident in the numerals of the questioned compared to the known writing.

Individual letters: Numerous individual letters are similar in the questioned and known material, both in shape and placement, as demonstrated in the comparison charts. Note especially the shape, terminal stroke and slant of lower case *d*; formation and terminal stroke of *h*; formation and final stroke of m; use of two different forms of *s* and the same shapes of each in both questioned and known; proportion and downward turn of *y* loop; construction and placement of individual words, including *and, had, he* and *Sheraton*.

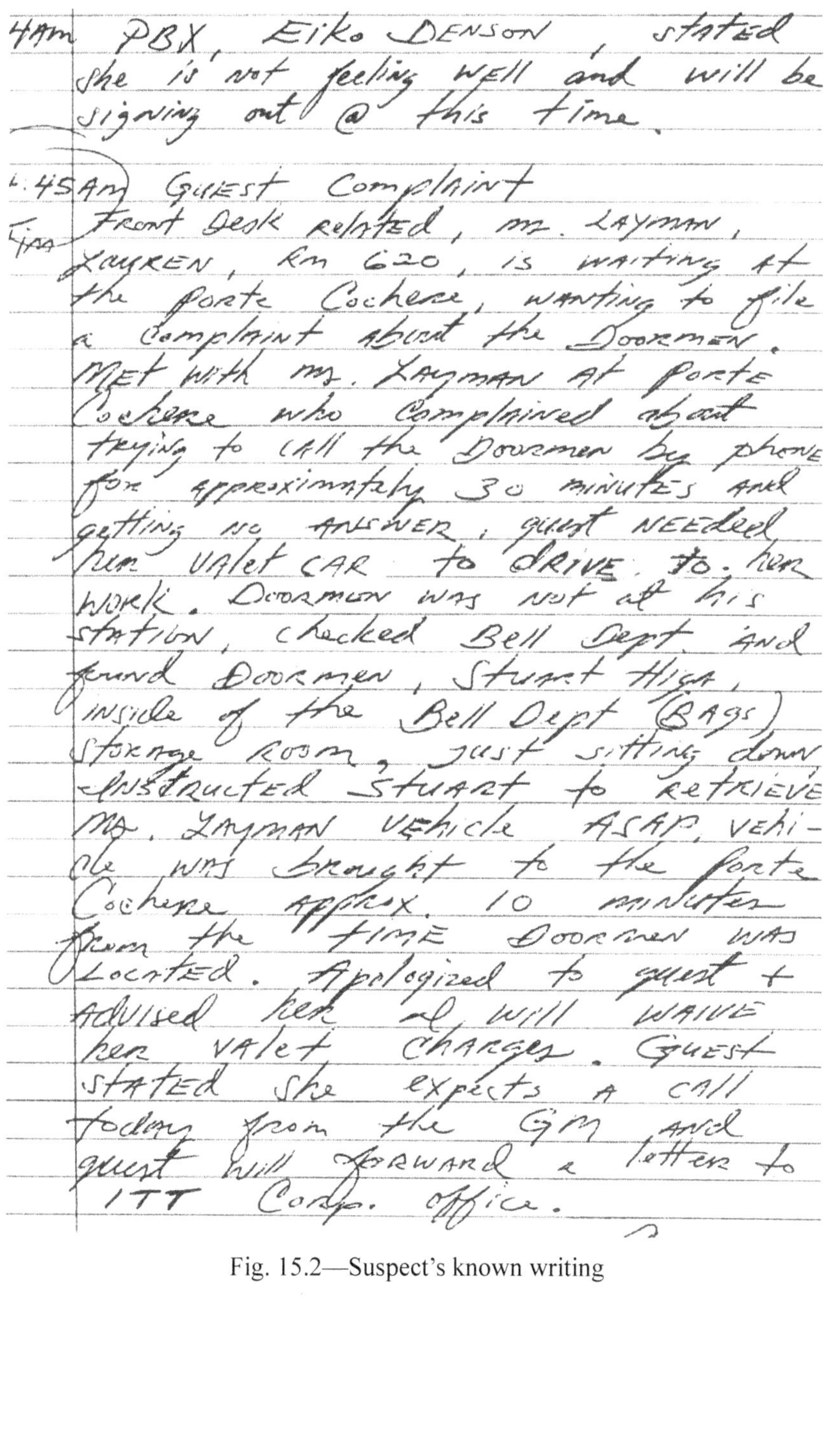

4AM PBX, Eiko DENSON, stated she is not feeling WELL and will be signing out @ this time.

4:45AM GUEST Complaint
Front Desk related, ms. LAYMAN, LAYREN, Rm 620, is waiting at the porte Cochere, wanting to file a Complaint about the Doormen. Met with ms. Layman at Porte Cochere who Complained about trying to call the Doormen by phone for approximately 30 minutes and getting no answer, guest needed her valet car to drive to her work. Doorman was not at his station, checked Bell Dept and found Doormen, Stuart High, inside of the Bell Dept (BAGS) Storage room, just sitting down. Instructed Stuart to retrieve ms. Layman vehicle ASAP. vehicle was brought to the porte Cochere approx. 10 minutes from the time Doormen was located. Apologized to guest + advised her I will waive her valet charges. Guest stated she expects a call today from the GM and guest will forward a letter to ITT Corp. office.

Fig. 15.2—Suspect's known writing

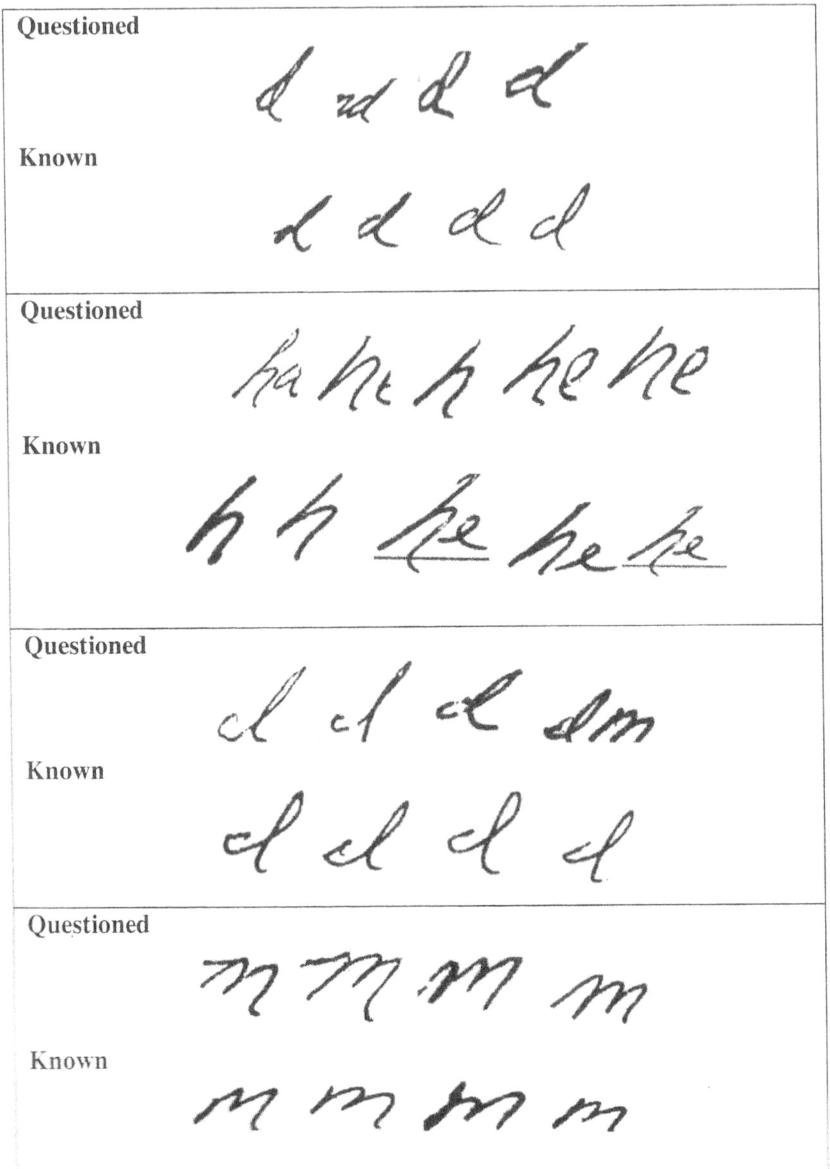

Fig. 15.3:—Comparison Chart 1

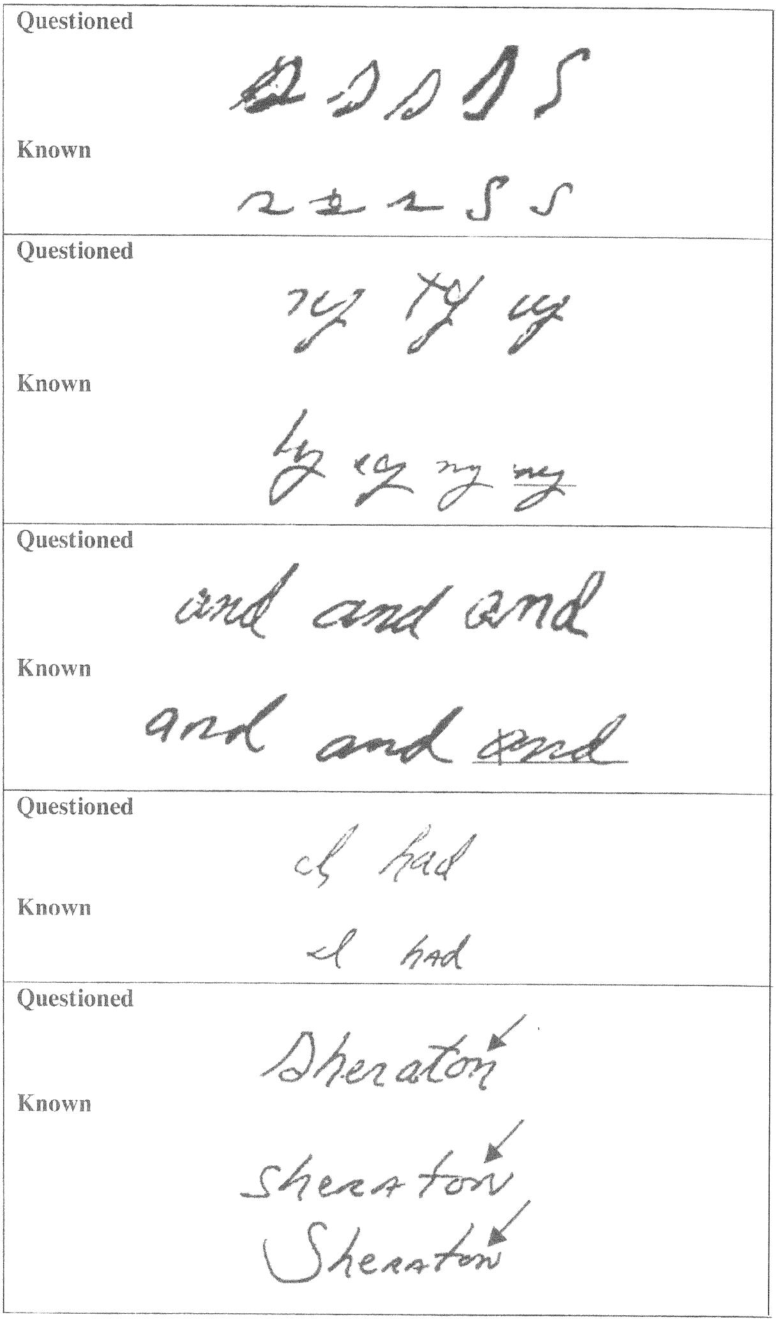

Fig. 15.4—Comparison Chart 2

Conclusion: The suspect's known writing is consistent with the postcard writing in many respects. There is similar arrangement in both, including a variable left margin and baselines that wander and droop toward the end. Proportions of upper and lower zone extenders are similar. There are unique connections in both, particularly the o-n movement in Sheraton. Word spacing is wide to extra wide and variable in each. Terminal strokes push forward and downward in both, usually with added pressure. Placement of periods is rather unique to the suspects writing and it repeats in the questioned material. Several individual letter formations are also the same in the questioned writing and that of the suspect, as shown in the comparison charts.

Epilogue: Given the number of similarities, it was concluded that the suspect did indeed author the anonymous postcard and that he apparently made an unsuccessful attempt at disguising his writing.

As a consequence to these findings and other information gathered by the security team at the hotel, the suspect was suspended. Subsequently, he filed a lawsuit against the hotel for wrongful termination. On the day before his trial was to begin, he suddenly withdrew charges against the hotel, admitting that he had authored the postcard and had also transmitted the additional questioned material.

16. Case History No. 3

This case is a post-divorce matter which involves the interests of a 12 year-old boy (hereinafter referred to as "Aaron Smith") who unfortunately suffers from cerebral palsy. Aaron's mother and father are now divorced and the mother is caring for Aaron on her own, with the assistance of tutors and health care providers.

In this case, Aaron's mother is filing a claim against her ex-husband in an attempt to prove that he is responsible for payment of some of Aaron's care. To support her claim she has produced numerous treatment notes and invoices allegedly from Aaron's providers.

However, there is some question as to the validity of the health care documentation and Mr. Smith's attorney has requested an examination of same. Along with the questioned material the attorney has provided various samples of Ms. Smith's handwriting and handprinting. He has requested an examination to determine, if possible, if the same person wrote both the questioned medical notes and invoices and whether Ms. Smith can be identified as the writer of either or both.

It is impossible to reproduce here all of the many pages of questioned and known handwriting that were furnished for the examination. However, it is believed that the material given is representative of the matter at hand.

Portions of two of the questioned documents are shown, followed by one sample of handwritten material and two samples of handprinting produced by Aaron's mother.

General observations: The questioned material consists of two allographs—handwriting on the medical notes and printing on the invoice. Note that some portions of the handwritten material is in a printscript style, especially the name Aaron. The questioned writing has a tenuous appearance in that the ductus is uncertain (for example, see the i in hospital and the first downstroke on n of stimulation). There are also conflicts in slant and letter formation. These are indications that the handwritten medical notes may have been disguised, but this warrants further investigation.

Although different allographs often cannot be successfully compared, there are apparent similarities between both questioned writings. In particular, the name Aaron and letters s and r, are similar in both the handwriting and printing. However, as initial impressions are not reliable, further comparison is necessary to determine if the invoice and medical notes are of common authorship.

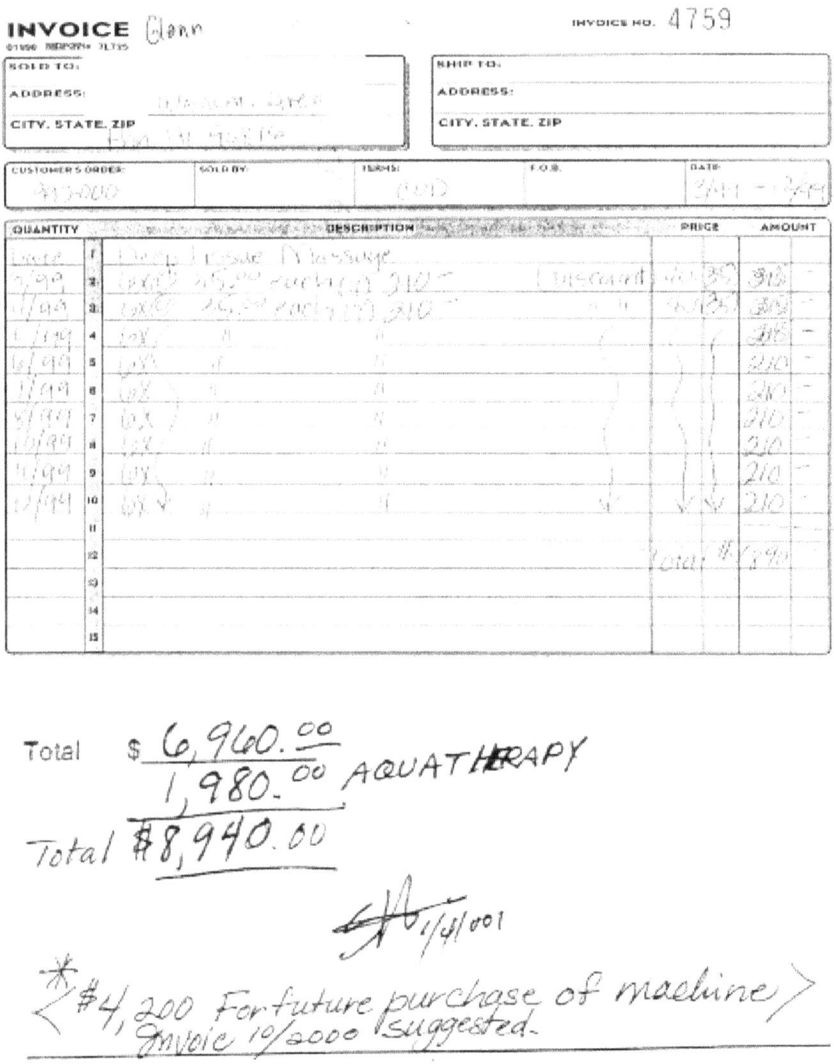

Fig. 16.1—Questioned documents

The known handwriting appears to be of a different style than the questioned writing; the questioned is more linear and simplified, while the known is generally more rounded and with some embellishment of initial and terminal strokes. The writer used two distinct printing styles, the second of which is a version of all capitals. The first known printing sample is very similar in appearance to the printing on the questioned invoice. The second printing exemplar appears heavier than the questioned invoice, although it seems that a broader pen was likely used to write the known. When compared closely, there are similarities with the printing on the questioned invoice.

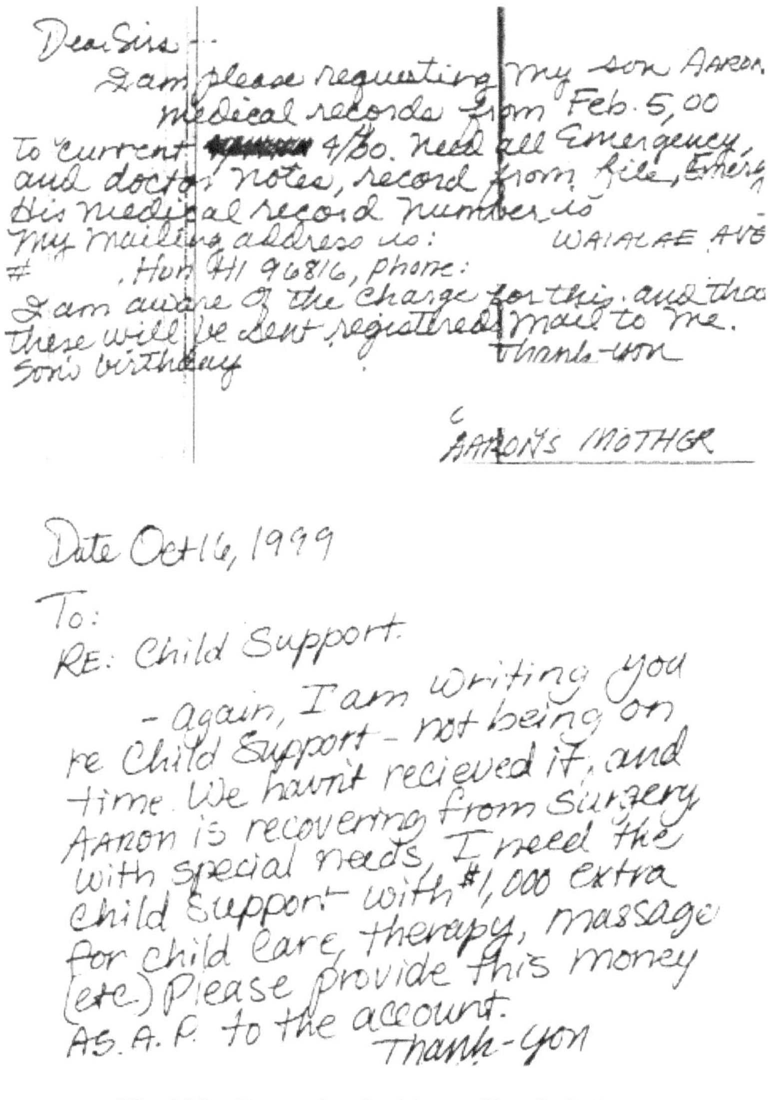
Dear Sirs -
I am please requesting my son AARON
medical records from Feb. 5, 00
To current 4/30. need all Emergency,
and doctor notes, record from file, Emerg
His medical record number is
My mailing address is: WAIALAE AVE
, Hon HI 96816, phone:
I am aware of the charge for this. and that
these will be sent registered mail to me.
Sons birthday thank-you
AARON'S MOTHER

Date Oct 16, 1999
To:
RE: Child Support.
- again, I am writing you
re Child Support - not being on
time. We havnt recieved it, and
AARON is recovering from surgery
with special needs, I need the
child support with #1,000 extra
for child care, therapy, massage
(etc.) Please provide this money
AS.A.P. to the account.
Thank-you

Fig. 16.2—Known handwriting and handprinting

Arrangement: Left and right margins of the questioned and known handwritings are similar in their slight variation although this is not an especially strong identifying feature and it cannot be relied upon as the margins of the questioned writing are somewhat restricted by the rulings on the paper. Line spacing cannot be compared for the same reason. Individualized arrangement of the printed material is also prevented to a certain extent by the lines and columns of the form itself.

Pressure: Pressure cannot be sufficiently evaluated as two of the known samples (especially the second printed sample) seem to have been produced with a wide tipped pen.

Spacing: Word spacing is similar in all writings when measured at the baseline and ignoring the initial embellishments in the questioned treatment notes which make the words look more closely spaced. (Similar word spacing is more apparent in other samples not illustrated here.)

Connecting strokes: The questioned writing is a combination of various connectors, as is the known handwriting. The known writing appears to be more rounded at first, but closer inspection shows considerable angularity. Connecting strokes are of course limited in the questioned and known printing. However, there is a distinctly similar connection in the *A-v* of the abbreviation Ave on the questioned invoice and the second printing exemplar. (See comparison charts.)

Initial and terminal strokes: The questioned writing is simplified and essentially without initial and terminal strokes. There are frequent hooks at the beginning of letters. The known handwriting also has initial hooks as well as numerous letters formed without lead-in strokes.

Slant: The slant of the known handwriting and printing is somewhat variable and slightly to the right. The questioned handwriting is slightly leftward, although on closer look it is variable and some upstrokes actually lean rightward. The printed samples are also variable in this regard.

Punctuation: Although not clearly shown in the samples given here, the formation and placement of punctuation is similar in both questioned and known handwriting and printing.

Numerals: The numbers in the questioned writing and printing are similar to each other and similar to the known handwriting which are similar to the known printing. Arrangement, placement, and formations of numbers are similar in all samples, as are formation and placement of commas after numbers, the use of a dash in the cents portion of dollar amounts and the use of slash marks between numbers. (See comparison charts below)

Signs and Symbols: Dollar signs and number signs are written in the same manner in all writings and are especially evident when comparing the questioned and known printing. Parentheses are also similar in shape and placement on the questioned invoice and the known handwriting sample.

Spelling: Although not shown here, the letterhead purporting to be from one of the medical providers displays the word *Tudor* instead of *Tutor*. This same spelling error is also noted in the second known printing sample. One would expect that a bona fide tutor would know how to spell the word correctly.

Individual letters: When individual letters of the questioned and known material are compared, numerous similarities are apparent, as evidenced in the comparison charts below. The capital letter *A* is revealing in that three different forms of the letter are utilized in both the questioned and known material. There are similar connections of the *A* to the letters that follow, particularly obvious in the abbreviation Ave and the name Aaron. This type of connection is to be noted in the capital *H* and letters that follow, especially noticeable in *H-i* and *H-o* connections. Note also that the cross bar of the *A* slants upward in nearly every instance.

Both capital and lower case *B* are of similar formation in all material examined. Capitals *C, D, F, H, I, P, S* and *W* are also similar.

The loops of the lower case g in both the questioned and known material are unfinished and cup-like.

While the style of lower case r is somewhat common and therefore not particularly revealing in itself, its relationship with the letter e is significant whether written as *e-r* or *r-e.*

The lower case *t* is frequently a simplified formation in both the questioned and known documentation. More revealing are the "tics" especially prevalent at the top of many ts and sometimes at the bottom. The angular formation at the base of the letter *t* is evident in all writings and is also repeated in the letter *f.*

Conclusions: The comparison charts included below clearly show similarities between the questioned material and the exemplars. There is no question that the first known printing sample was authored by the person who wrote the questioned invoice. Numerous similarities are apparent, including letter proportions, letter and word spacing, use of numbers and slash marks. Therefore, the author of the questioned invoice is the same person who authored the first known printing sample.

Numbers in the second printed sample are quite similar to those used on the questioned invoice, as are individual letters (especially *A*). Arrangement of the name Aaron and formation of the letter r in that word are remarkably similar. Note also the same type of connector used in *H-i* on the questioned printing and the H-u connector in the second known printing sample. Therefore, the author of the second known printing sample also authored the questioned invoice. This confirms (although it has already been alleged) that the same person authored both known printing samples.

Numerous individual features of the questioned handwriting match those of the writer of the known handwriting sample as reflected in the comparison charts. Especially noteworthy are the word of, lower case *p*, lower case g, lower case *s*, capital *H*, and capital *A*.

Highly significant are the commonalities between the name Aaron on the questioned invoice, the questioned handwriting and the second known printing sample. As shown in the comparison charts, other even closer matches were discovered in this word when comparing questioned to known. The icing on the cake in this case is the misspelled word Tudor which appears on several fabricated letterheads and in the handwritten material produced by Ms. Smith.

Based on all of the above, it becomes apparent that the same person who authored the three exemplary samples also wrote both the questioned treatment notes and questioned invoice.

Epilogue: Armed with this information and even more extensive comparison charts than those illustrated here, Mr. Smith's attorney intended to call me as an expert witness at trial in this case to help prove that Ms. Smith had fabricated numerous doctors' notes, treatment records and invoices, all in an effort to obtain money from her estranged husband. Given the solidity of the handwriting findings, the judge would not allow the matter to proceed to trial and, instead, forced the parties to settle out of court.

Questioned:

Q-3A Q-3B Q-2

Known:

K-2 K-3 K-3

K-2

Questioned:

Q-1L Q-1P Q-1R Q-2 Q-2 Q-4 Q-4

Known:

K-5 K-3 K-1 K-4 K-4 K-4 K-4

Questioned:

Q-1W Q-1Q

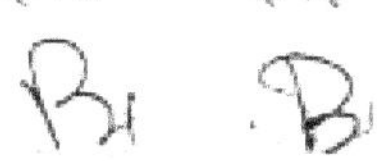

Known:

K-4 K-4 K-5

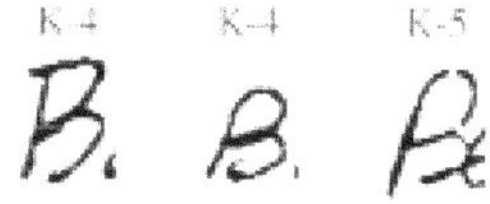

Questioned:

Q-1H Q-1H Q-1I Q-1J Q-1S Q-1N Q-1V Q-1W

Known:

K-1 K-5 K-10 K-10

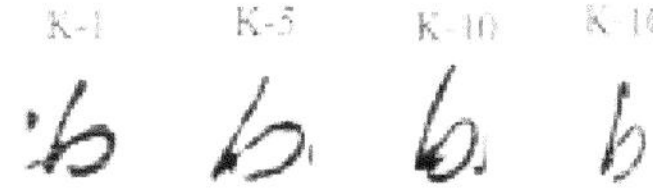

Questioned

TUDOR Tudor

Known

Questioned:

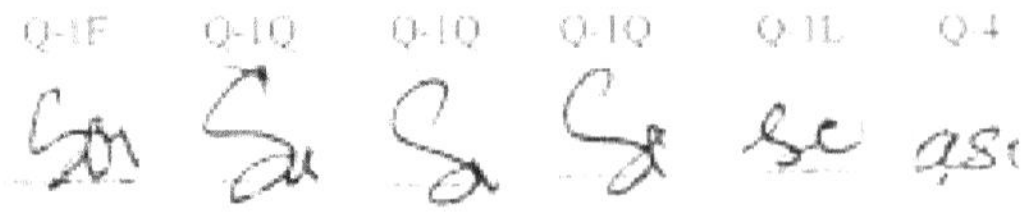

Known:

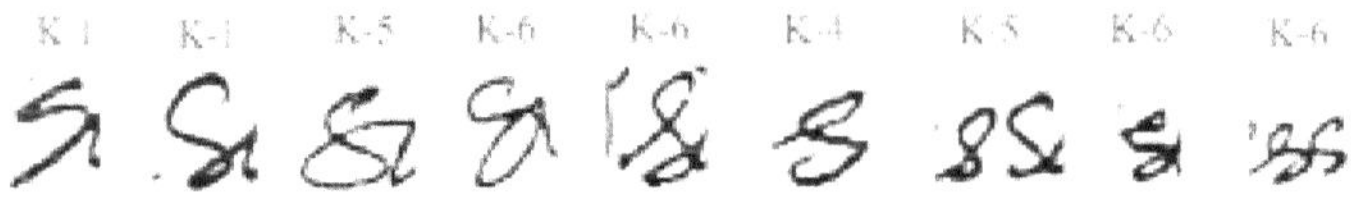

Questioned:

Known:

Questioned:

Known:

Questioned:

Known:

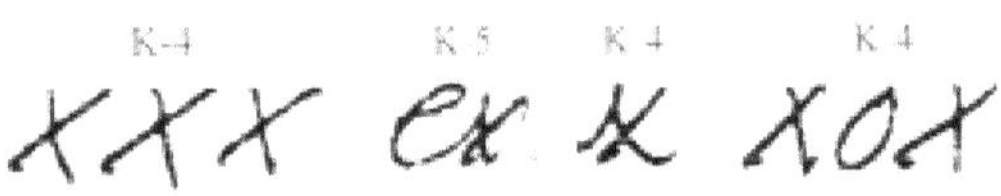

17. Rendering Opinions

Opinions are an integral part of the forensic handwriting examination process. As summaries of an expert's conclusions, they are paramount to the resolution of disputed writing matters. As will be discussed later in this chapter, written reports are particularly important as they often become part of a permanent court record.

Degrees of Opinion

Depending on the nature of the case at hand and the material presented for examination, opinions vary in degree from absolute certainty on the one hand to absolute uncertainty on the other. Because they are based on the analyst's individual examination and the evidence presented, rather than statistics or quantitative data, opinions are not easily classified under percentages of certainty.

Until somewhat recently, there has been relatively little consensus as to the manner of expressing qualified opinions in handwriting and document cases. However, thanks largely to the efforts of document examiner Thomas McAlexander, standard terminology has been adopted by the Questioned Document Section of the American Academy of Forensic Sciences and the ASTM (American Standards and Testing Materials).[1]

The dictionary defines absolute as "free from any restriction or limitation or exception...Positive, certain: absolute in opinion." For various reasons handwriting and document conclusions cannot always be absolute. It is disconcerting to know that some examiners are able to render a definite conclusion on every case they handle. There is equal concern about those who habitually reach inconclusive opinions, even when examining adequate material, as constant indecision tends to reflect negatively on the profession.

Harrison wrote that "the most definite opinion expressed by any document examiner is subject to the unspoken qualification 'as far as my skill allows,' for unless he saw a specimen of handwriting being written, he is unable to swear to its authorship however skilled he may be."[2]

Conclusions that are less than absolute can, however, be acceptable

---

1. Thomas V. McAlexander, "A Layman's Guide to Handwriting Opinion Terminology," The Police Chief, May 1978.
2. Wilson Harrison, *Suspect Documents,* Chicago: Nelson-Hall Publishers, 1981, p.346.

as part of the expert's testimony. In fact, experts are not retained to reach a decision one way or another. Instead, they are hired to find the truth as it exists in the documents presented for examination and to render observations and opinions based on their knowledge and expertise. If the examiner's opinions are supportive of the client's position, so much the better, but the expert should avoid reaching the opinion he or she thinks the client is after because of the pay involved or (in the case of some novice examiners) the hope of acquiring courtroom experience.

A seasoned examiner will not publish any opinion stronger than that which can be effectively demonstrated. Clients are entitled to conclusions that can be proven and, if they cannot be proven, they should be given explanations why.

It is suggested that the expert play devil's advocate and look at each case as the opposition might. If a case can be made for either side, the opinions must be qualified or rendered as inconclusive. (Playing devil's advocate also helps prepare for questions the opposition will likely ask at deposition or on cross-examination.)

Qualified opinions should be expressed as such and the wording of the opinion should correspond to the weight of the evidence. A strong opinion might be weakened or misunderstood due to the language of the report. On the other hand, a qualified opinion, if written improperly, might place the expert in an embarrassing position with the client if the opinion is misinterpreted as a more certain conclusion. In other words, the expert is admonished to say exactly what is intended.

The following degrees of opinion are utilized by handwriting experts in rendering reports.

Absolute—An absolute or definite conclusion reflects the highest degree of certainty. Given the material provided for the examination, the expert has no question about the conclusion. There are no qualifications or reservations on the part of the examiner and he or she will be able to demonstrate why there is no uncertainty.

A positive identification essentially states that there are no fundamental differences between two writings outside the scope of natural variation. There may be some slight differences, but the reasons for such differences can be explained. Such reasoning might include natural variation, the effect of medication, writing while riding in a vehicle, writing on a rough surface, writing while lying down or use of a faulty pen.

Absolute conclusions may be expressed as It is my professional opinion that...

- the writer of K1 also wrote signature Q1.
- the writer of K1 is the same person who (signed, wrote, endorsed) Q1.
- the (signature, writing, endorsement) on Q1 was written by the author of K1.
- writing Q1 and K1 are of common authorship.
- all the identifiable writing characteristics contained in Q1 are also present in K1; therefore, a positive identification of a common authorship exists.

These absolute positives can be altered to absolute negatives such as *It is my professional opinion that the signature on Q1 is not genuine.*

Highly probable—This area includes "almost positive" opinions. While the examiner may be quite certain in the identification or elimination of a writer, an unequivocal opinion cannot be rendered due to some condition(s) in the writings or documents which are unexplainable.

Highly probable opinions might be stated as *It is highly probable that Q1 was (signed, endorsed, written) by the same person who authored K1. However...*

- due to the limited amount of questioned material (or standards) submitted, a positive identification cannot be established.
- original material was unavailable for the examination which prevents a definite conclusion.
- there are dissimilarities between K1 and Q1 that cannot be explained; therefore, a positive identification cannot be reached.
- the existence of unnatural writing in Q1 precludes a positive identification.
- the conditions (intoxication, drugs, illness, any transitory condition) under which Q1 were allegedly written prevent a positive conclusion.
- the non contemporaneous dating of (Q1, K1) and (Q1, K1) preclude a positive identification due to possible change in the writing over time.

Probable—Some examiners prefer not to express opinions in this range, but in some cases a probable opinion can be most appropriate. For instance, if the questioned material is composed of a series of names, words or numbers on one page, it might be a relatively easy task for the examiner to render a positive identification on most of the names, words or numbers. But there might be some items which, standing alone, do not conform to the exemplars. In this case the expert would render a positive conclusion regarding only certain entries on the document. However, since all the questioned items appear on the same page, it would be a reasonable deduction that those items not conforming to the standards were *probably* all written by the same person who wrote the other entries.

Probable opinions might be stated as:

- The writer of K1 probably (signed, wrote, endorsed) Q1.
- The writer of K1 should not be eliminated as the probable writer of Q1.
- There is evidence to suggest that the writer of K1 also (signed, wrote, endorsed) Q1.
- There are common writing characteristics in K1 and Q1 that suggest the probability of common authorship.
- While there is insufficient information to render a positive identification, there is ample evidence to conclude that Q1 was probably written by the author of K1.

Inconclusive—Rendering an inconclusive opinion does not in any way reflect upon the handwriting examiner's competence, unless he or she is simply too lazy to do the work or too afraid of standing up to what is believed to be true.

Oftentimes it is more appropriate to render an inconclusive opinion than risk an incorrect conclusion that could adversely affect an innocent party.

Factors involving the documents such as condition, questionable origin, illegibility or dating may prevent even the most competent examiner from reaching a certain conclusion. When unable to reach a conclusive opinion, the client should be given justification for why the examiner cannot be more certain.

Inconclusive opinions may be expressed such as *The writer of K1 can neither be identified or eliminated as the writer of Q1 due to...*

- the apparent use of disguise.
- the document having been written under the influence of drugs or alcohol.
- lack of contemporaneous standards.
- poor (condition, quality, legibility) of (copies, writing).
- improper allographs for comparison (e.g., print compared to script).
- lack of sufficient identifiable characteristics in the questioned (signature, writing, numbers).
- abbreviated material such as one number or a very short signature.

Written Reports

Once opinions have been reached in handwriting cases, they are often reported in writing. Reports or letters of opinion frequently become part of a court record at some point in the litigation process and it is therefore imperative that the final product be accurate and professional in every respect.

When writing reports it is important that the examiner use terms that are fully understandable to the client and, ultimately, the trier of fact. The terminology utilized must project the intended meaning. Technical jargon should be avoided, unless accompanied by definitions so that there is no question as to what is being expressed. It is generally best to write in commonly understandable terms. Care must be taken to avoid anything that will result in a position of having to defend one's opinions with statements like "but that's not exactly what I meant!"

The opinion letter plays a significant role in conveying the examiner's professionalism. And, as the expert will likely be called upon to testify as to its content and accuracy, the report should be soundly presented. Any mistakes can of course be admitted while on the witness stand, but that opens wide the door for attack on the rest of the report.

The expert must carefully select the words or phrases that accurately define the intended meaning. Opinions that are overdone, flowery or too wordy may jeopardize the value of the report and, worse, the outcome of the case in question. Simple is always better than complex.

Before writing a report the expert will of course have to reach opinions and be thoroughly familiar with the reasoning behind them. However, prior to committing opinions to paper, the client should be queried as to whether he or she wants the opinion in writing. If the examiner's conclusion does not support the position the client had hoped for, it is not likely that they will want it committed to writing. Anything written is of course discoverable by the opposition, which the attorney or client may wish to avoid.

Once the report has been obtained by the opposition, it can then be presented to an opposing document examiner, if one has been retained. The opposing examiner will dissect the report, looking for flaws in reasoning and conclusions which will give the other side ammunition to be used at deposition or in court. In some cases examiners are retained merely to scrutinize another expert's report for rebuttal purposes.

In some jurisdictions experts may testify only to information contained in their reports. It is therefore advisable to cover everything pertinent to the case at issue, including any bases for conclusions as well as indication of any similarities or dissimilarities the expert expects to explain at trial. Prior to trial, opposing counsel may file a *Motion in Limine* which, if granted, will prevent the expert from testifying to anything not included in the report.

With respect to federal cases, complete reports are required. Reasoning behind conclusions must be included as well as any demonstrative material which evidences the soundness of those conclusions.

General report format

There are variables in handwriting related cases so that each report will depend to a certain extent on the situation at hand. However, some guidelines are in order.

The examiner must strive to use concise, professional writing, double checking that the report has been correctly dated and addressed and the case name and/or number has been referenced. The report should of course appear on professional letterhead. Reports that extend into several pages, especially if they include comparison charts, may be placed into loose leaf binders or held together at the top by fasteners.

The first paragraph often indicates the date of initial contact, how the documents were received and who issued and/or delivered them for the examination. Here the examiner may briefly state the nature of the problem at hand, using such statements as *You have indicated that the 'John Smith' signature on the contract dated 12/2/04 is under investigation as to authenticity or You have provided document X, indicating that the handwritten material on said document is being questioned as to authenticity.*

These sections follow the introductory paragraph:

Questioned Material

In this section the questioned documents (or signatures or handwriting) are listed so that they can be easily identified by anyone who reads the report. It is recommended that they be referred to by number (Q1, Q2, etc.) for ease of reference. Wherever possible, the actual title of any documents should be used. If a document has no title, describe it in such a way that it can be easily distinguished from other documents. If the document consists of more than one page, indicate the page number(s) bearing the questioned handwriting.

It is helpful to attach to the report, as exhibits, a copy of every document examined so that, again, there is no doubt as to what has been evaluated. Numbering any attached exhibits allows them to be referred to easily both by the reader and the examiner during testimony.

Exemplars / Comparison Standards

Here the examiner lists all documents bearing the handwriting standards used in the examination. As with the questioned material, it is important to number the exemplary documents, refer to them by title and/or describe them in detail so that they can be easily identified. With multiple-page documents, indicate the number of total pages and note on which page the exemplar appears. In identifying numbered items such as checks, use the proper number, and keep all items consecutive numerically or chronologically. Copies of all standards should be attached as exhibits to the report and labeled appropriately.

Assignment

This section contains a brief description of what the client requested. *(You have requested a comparison of signature Q with the known signatures provided, in an effort to determine authenticity or You have asked that I determine the author or source of the handwriting in question.)*

Procedure / Method of Examination

Here the examiner describes the steps taken in reaching any conclusions. *(In accordance with your request... or Pursuant to your request...I have done such and such. I enlarged the questioned and known signatures by 150% for ease of comparison. I viewed the signature under various degrees of magnification. I examined the signature microscopically. I utilized ultraviolet lighting to determine the presence of erasures or to compare types of paper.)*

Opinions / Conclusions / Findings From Examination

This is where opinions about the signature, handwriting or document in question are spelled out. *(Following my examination of the comparison material, I have reached the following opinions... or Based on reasonable scientific certainty, it is my opinion that... or Based upon reasonable technical and scientific methods, I have concluded that...)*

When rendering multiple opinions, more clarity will be attained by setting the conclusions apart by starting each new paragraph with *"Opinion:"*. Bullets or numbers may be used instead. Underlining or italicizing the one line that concisely states the conclusion is also helpful to the reader. *(I am of the opinion that the writer of the John Brown exemplar signatures also authored the signature in question.)*

At this point it is advisable to explain why and how conclusions have been reached, otherwise they have no plausible foundation. As always, the expert should consider that he or she will likely be questioned by opposing counsel about any opinions or the reasoning behind them.

Some examiners choose not to report the basis for their conclusions, thinking this gives the opposition added material to attack at deposition. However, one may be equally questioned about not giving a reason or giving a flimsy reason for any findings. Further, the client deserves to know what is logical and reasonable with respect to the issue at hand, as opposed to simply being given non-supported conclusions.

Additional Comments

In the final paragraphs of the report the examiner may explain or comment upon anything that is not specific to the immediate matter, but which may be peripherally important or of interest to the client.

In this section the examiner may indicate how the documents are being returned to the client. If any of the documentation is being retained for whatever reason (as for preparing courtroom exhibits), this should be addressed with a comment such as "pending further instructions." A courteous conclusion is often added. *(Please contact me at your earliest convenience should you wish me to testify to these findings or Feel free to contact me with any questions or concerns.)*

Some document examiners include in their reports statements like, *The basis for the opinion(s) expressed herein can be demonstrated in a court of law.* Most experts recommended avoiding use of the word prove in place of demonstrate. Demonstrating the basis for opinions at a hearing or in trial should not be difficult, but indicating that conclusions can be proven may be overstating one's capabilities. After all, it is the trier of fact (the judge or jury) who ultimately determines the value of courtroom testimony and demonstration.

Comparison Charts / Visual Aids

To make one's position patently clear, it is recommended that comparison charts or other visual aids be attached. They allow anyone reading the report to readily visualize the differences or similarities upon which conclusions are based and they can be effectively utilized when explaining material to the client, his or her counsel, the opposing attorney and/or judge.

Additional tips

The examiner would be wise to steer clear of the word fact when rendering any opinion. *(The writing was in fact not written by so-and-so or The signature was in fact forged.)* Unless the writing was actually witnessed by the examiner, he or she cannot know for sure. Superlatives like certain, always, never or absolute should also be avoided. *(The suspect never writes his capital B in that way is not recommended.)* There is an exception to every rule and the opposition will look for it. A better statement is *The preponderance of similarities indicates...*

Some document examiners suggest that actual names of suspects not be incorporated into conclusions, like *John Smith is the author of document Q1.* It is generally better to state something like, *I have concluded that the author of Q1 is the same person who wrote K1.* This gives the same conclusion but does not bind the expert to a specific suspect. Consider, for example, the possibility that K1 might not actually have been written by the person named in the report as led to believe. Now the examiner is faced with having possibly accused an innocent party.

Opinions Based on Photocopies or Facsimiles

When examining a photocopied or faxed document containing what is believed to be a genuine signature, it is wise to state that although the signature appears to be authentic, without the original it cannot be concluded that the signature was originally placed on that specific document. Such an explanation would take into account the possibility of a cut and paste signature on a photocopy or computer generated document.

It is suggested that the examiner include a qualifying disclaimer in any report of a document job involving photocopied, faxed, electronically produced or computer generated material. Such a disclaimer might read:

- Based upon the evidence (or documents) submitted (or examined), I conclude such and such.
- Opinions based on the examination of photocopies are subject to revision should I examine original documentation at a later date.
- I reserve the right to amend my findings and conclusions upon the examination of the original document.

18. The Handwriting Expert As Witness

The purpose of the handwriting examiner's testimony is to assist the judge, court or jury in understanding the facts regarding those technical parts of evidence about which he or she possesses special knowledge.

Usually the expert appears on behalf of one of the litigants, but technically should not be biased toward either party's cause. Instead, the examiner is to seek the truth as evidenced by the documentation at issue, which truth is then presented to the court. The examiner must be fair, ethical and unbiased at all times else he or she will not be acting in the interest of justice.

Generally a handwriting witness appears through agreement with counsel for the client for whom the work has been performed, although there are instances when the opposition issues a subpoena for the examiner to appear. One must honor any subpoena, whether it be a *subpoena duces tecum* normally issued for the purpose of examining the expert's entire file, or a subpoena to appear in court to render testimony. A judge can deem a witness in contempt if a subpoena is ignored.

According to Osborn, "To be effective as a witness the specialist must not only know, but must be able to explain, to convince, and to undergo cross-examination. For his own protection, as well as to increase the effectiveness of his testimony, he must know these things and understand what conditions and qualities strengthen or weaken the technical evidence of a specialist."[1]

As Osborn points out, to testify effectively the examiner must understand his or her specialty as well as how and for what reasons any conclusions have been reached. Additionally, one's findings must be explained in such a way that will be fully understandable by the judge or jury. Testimony is effective when it is clear, forceful and presented with confidence, which will of course be convincing to the trier of fact. More importantly, one's testimony must be the truth.

Preparation for Trial

Prior to appearing in court or rendering testimony at deposition, the examiner will of course have reached conclusions pertaining to the case at hand. These conclusions must be thoroughly discussed at a confer-

1. Albert Osborn, *The Problem of Proof,* Albany, NY: The Boyd Printing Company, 1946.

ence with the client's attorney in advance of trial, along with the how and why of those conclusions.

The pretrial meeting will help the expert better understand the case from the attorney's standpoint and, more importantly, will clarify what is expected of him or her while on the witness stand. It is an opportunity for both counsel and expert to strategize their approach and to cover anything that will likely be brought out at trial with respect to the handwriting at issue. At this time the examiner will have a chance to educate the attorney regarding handwriting identification which will facilitate the presentation of this part of the case in the courtroom.

The pretrial conference is an opportunity to rehearse the explanation of the expert's examination and findings as if he were actually on the witness stand. It is also a chance for counsel to address any potential problem areas and questions that are apt to come up during cross-examination by the opposition. The examiner should inform counsel of any weak spots related to the handwriting issue, so that they will both be prepared to deal with any attacks by the opposition.

The expert's report should be considered in detail at this meeting, in anticipation of questions from the other side. Any photos or demonstrative charts should also be carefully reviewed.

It is recommended that at this time the examiner furnish counsel with a list of standard questions and answers regarding training and experience for the purpose of guiding the witness qualification process as discussed below.

Admissibility of Expert Testimony

Opinions of expert witnesses are admitted into evidence on the theory that they are necessary to justice. Consequently, the following questions arise when an expert is called: 1) Is the subject matter of significance to the issue at hand? 2) What qualifications are necessary to enable the expert to testify on the subject? and 3) Does the witness meet those qualifications?

It is the court who answers these questions at its own discretion. Every time the examiner is called to give testimony at trial, he or she must be newly qualified by the judge hearing that particular case.

The generally accepted rule is that a person is an expert when he or she has special knowledge, skill or practical experience in a particular area, which knowledge is beyond the training or knowledge of the layperson and has been acquired by scientific, professional and/or technical training and experience. The court (not the jury) decides if the expert does in fact measure up with respect to background and experience in his or her area of expertise.

Depositions

When a lawsuit is filed, the parties to the suit are entitled to the process of discovery. This enables the litigants to be apprised of any information held by the opposition. Any witnesses must be disclosed, along with their findings which assists the parties to better determine the merits of the case.

As part of the discovery process, depositions are witness interviews taken out of court, usually in the conference room of one of the attorneys involved. They are generally arranged by the opposing party as part of the discovery process in a lawsuit, for the purpose of determining how much the expert knows about the case, what his or her conclusions are, and how those conclusions were reached.

Although less formal than courtroom testimony, depositions are nevertheless equally serious. They are taken under oath and the proceedings are recorded by a court reporter. In most instances, lawyers from both sides are present along with their respective clients.

As with trial testimony, the deposing attorney is allowed to question the witness regarding qualifications, background, education, experience and, of course, the matter at hand. The deposition is a "fishing trip" of sorts as it allows the opposition to search for anything that might be pertinent to the case. It also allows opposing counsel to discover any vulnerability in the witness or his testimony. It gives the opposition a chance to see how the witness will likely appear at trial, whether he will make a good impression and how he can be discredited. If a witness changes his or her testimony between deposition and trial, their credibility will surely be challenged on the witness stand, unless there is a very sound reason for the shift in opinion.

In many cases depositions are more harrowing than actual courtroom appearances because although the deponent's attorney may object to certain lines of questioning "for the record," the witness is nevertheless required to answer. The opposition may require the witness to bring to the deposition material only possibly related to the issue at hand, such as copies of document examination texts, any publications the expert has authored and, in some instances, equipment used in the examination like microscopes and measuring devices.

In most cases depositions extend for a longer span of time than actual courtroom appearances. They usually cover a broader range of material and consequently can be tiring to the witness. If the expert becomes fatigued or hungry, he can ask for a break and will usually be accommodated.

Once it has been prepared by the court reporter, a transcript of the proceedings is provided to the witness/deponent so that any errors can be corrected. At this time the deponent should not re-write the transcript, but merely change any glaring mistakes. The transcript should be thoroughly reviewed before trial as opposing counsel will have studied it for any inconsistencies. Anything the expert says during deposition may be brought out at trial.

Depositions are to be handled in essentially the same way a witness tackles actual courtroom testimony. The witness must be professional and ethical in every respect.

Rendering Testimony at Trial

One's testimony is carried out in phases starting with the witness being qualified by the judge. Direct examination is then conducted by the retaining attorney, followed by cross-examination by opposing counsel. The retaining attorney may then conduct a re-direct examination to clarify any points and/or rehabilitate the witness after the opposition has done his work. This may then be followed by opposing counsel's further cross-examination ("re-cross").

Qualification

The qualification process (called *voir dire*) normally begins with the retaining attorney asking questions of the expert (for the benefit of the judge) regarding background, training, experience, work history, professional affiliations, publications and expertise with respect to the matter at hand. Opposing counsel is then allowed to interview the expert as well, usually with an eye toward impeachment so that the judge will not allow testimony. Witness disqualification may be based on insufficient training or knowledge about the matter currently at issue, lack of mental ability, a reputation for perjury or previous conviction for a crime.

The expert's curriculum vitae (CV) will have been issued by this time, a copy of which will likely be in the hands of opposing counsel as well as the judge. The judge will review the CV for qualifications, while the opposition will usually attempt to find flaws in it. It is imperative that the CV be accurate and professional as recommended in Chapter 19 and the expert should expect to be questioned about anything that is presented in it.

If after *voir dire* the judge is satisfied that the examiner meets the established criteria, the examiner will then be qualified as an expert in that particular case. It is possible that the witness will be qualified only in one specific area. For example, he or she may not be qualified to render testimony about the chemistry of ink due to lack of experience in that area, but will be qualified to testify as to the examination of signatures.

Occasionally opposing counsel will choose to stipulate to the expert's qualifications rather than performing an interrogation about training and background. If, for example, the expert has previously done work for opposing counsel, the opposition is already familiar with the examiner's practices and experience and may want to dispense with the questioning phase. This tactic may seem to be in the interest of saving valuable court time and it of course prevents added stress on the witness, but it does not allow the jury to hear about the examiner's knowledge, expertise and accomplishments, which may factor into credibility.

Direct examination

Once the expert is qualified by the judge, direct examination is conducted by his attorney. Direct testimony essentially consists of two parts. First, there are introductory questions which lead up to and include the expert's opinion. (What documents did you examine? For what purpose did you examine the documents? Have you arrived at an opinion in that regard? What is that opinion?)

Second, the expert is questioned as to reasoning for any conclusions. It is during the second phase that the expert is normally asked to demonstrate his findings, usually by utilizing comparison charts or other visual aids. This is an opportunity to teach the court or jury about the dynamics of handwriting and why it is that no two people write alike.

It is generally recommended that during the initial phase the expert summarize the reasons for opinions by referring to such writing features as speed, line quality, skill and individual writing habits, reminding the jury that each part adds to the whole and that the sum is more significant than its individual components. In the final phase of direct examination, the witness can then return to those individual features and explain them more meaningfully by way of demonstrative material.

The seasoned attorney will find a way to have his witness repeat conclusions more than once so that they will be impressed upon jurors' minds.

Cross-examination

During cross-examination the handwriting expert should be prepared to have their qualifications, methods and findings thoroughly challenged by opposing counsel. In fact, the dictionary defines cross-examination as "to question a witness called by the other party in a court of law to *discredit or undercut testimony already given.*" (Emphasis added.)

This procedure can be disconcerting for even the most experienced witness. However, understanding typical cross-examination tactics and learning how best to respond can be helpful. The expert should strive to remain calm and collected, no matter how frustrated. He or she should always take time when answering questions, considering exactly what has been asked and answering just that without offering further information.

An air of modest confidence is impressive to jurors, while arrogance or ignorance are certain to undermine presentation of even the best evidence.

Methods employed by cross-examining attorneys are generally straight-forward, but often they include insinuations or downright abuse and insult. Opposing counsel may be seemingly congenial and professional or overtly hostile. No matter what attitude, they are always to be considered the opposition who is attempting to discredit the expert and what he intends to prove.

One cross-examination tactic is to irritate the witness so that he or she snaps back with impulsive responses which are sometimes contradictory to what was testified earlier. The remedy is of course to maintain poise and an air of professionalism.

Opposing attorneys sometimes ask the witness to review material on which several names are written, insisting that he or she make an on-the-spot determination as to whether the names were written by one person and, if produced by more than one person, who wrote what. The witness would of course refuse the challenge, citing reasons why the examination process is not that simple, particularly considering improper comparison material and the unavailability of one's usual examination equipment.

Frequently opposing attorneys do their homework by locating books by Osborn or Hilton at the local law library and reading up on the principles and procedures of document examination. Of course they will not come into the courtroom with a full understanding of the subject, but will surely be armed with some bit of information intended to trip up the expert. There may be a line of questioning such as, "Ms. Smith, are you familiar with such-and-such publication? Do you agree that the author is an expert in your field? Is it not true that the author states such-and-such, and isn't it true that contradicts what you have told the court?" Obviously this approach is designed to discredit one's testimony by challenging knowledge and familiarity with the matter at hand.

Should the opposition quote a passage from a document examination text, the witness may want to ask to hear what appears before and after that passage. Material taken out of context can often be misconstrued, which may be exactly what opposing counsel intends.

Hypothetical questions are often posed during cross-examination, usually in an effort to get the witness to admit something that does not apply to the case at hand. When answering any hypotheticals, the expert should qualify the response with "Yes, hypothetically" or "If that were the case" or "Yes, in some instances" or "To a degree" or "It depends."

Often the intent of the cross-examining attorney is to confuse the witness, the jury or both. With this objective in mind, the attorney may induce statements that are damaging to the expert's professionalism or the issues that are being supported.

Sometimes the cross-examiner harps on incompetence by asking the expert things like, "Did you have all of the facts necessary to work this case?" or "Did you think to consider such-and-such?" Sufficient comparison material will assist in answering the former and using a standard examination process will help deal with the latter.

Cross-examining attorneys sometimes ask compound or confusing questions. The witness will certainly look more level headed with a polite request for clarification rather than attempting to respond to the unanswerable. When and if there is any doubt, the expert may preface the response with, "If I understand you correctly…"

The expert has the right to say that a yes or no answer would be misleading and should say so if a categorical answer is inaccurate. If the witness is restricted by the cross-examiner from giving a full answer, a more complete explanation will hopefully be elicited during the re-direct phase of testimony.

It is important that the witness stick to the question posed and not express more than is called for. The more information given to opposing counsel, the more fuel there will be for interrogation. At the same time, the expert may not avoid answering or deliberately hide any information, which would surely be perceived negatively by the jury. At all times the truth must be told. In no case should the expert express bias, even if an answer seems damaging to his own client.

If the expert also performs character analyses via graphology or Graphoanalysis™, that fact will likely be brought out at trial. Opposing counsel may attempt to impeach the witness by claiming that he or she dabbles in a craft that has no scientific merit and therefore the judge should disallow testimony. An effective way to defuse the opposition in this regard is to have the matter brought out during direct examination. The witness can then explain that graphology is essentially looking at the same intricate details of writing, but for a different purpose than the forensic examination. Also, it can be stated that graphology was not used in working the present case. A forensic examiner who also studies or uses handwriting for character profiling is no different than someone who plays both baseball and tennis.

Possible cross-examination questions include the following:

- What full time training have you undertaken to qualify you as an expert?
- Do you consider yourself a full time examiner of questioned documents? If not, what else do you do and how many hours do you spend on handwriting work?
- Have you ever worked in a document examination laboratory?
- How many questioned documents have you examined?

- How many do you examine a year?
- Have any of your cases been supervised?
- In what percentage of cases are you able to make a positive identification of handwriting?
- In what percentage of cases have you been unable to make a positive identification?
- What percentage of accuracy do you maintain?
- Have you ever reached an incorrect opinion?
- What leading texts in this field do you have in your library?
- What are some of the principle methods used to detect a deliberately disguised handwriting?
- Can you explain the theory of handwriting identification?
- Please describe the method you follow in a disputed handwriting case to determine whether the writing is genuine or forged.
- How long does it take you to decide whether a signature is genuine?
- How many exemplars do you need to make a comparison of handwriting?
- How many similarities are required to identify a writer?
- Is it easier to identify or eliminate a writer?

If the expert is unprepared or not fully qualified, vigorous cross-examination can be anticipated. Even if the expert is more seasoned, thorough cross-examination should be expected, but the ordeal gradually becomes less stressful with experience. In any case, the expert should expect the unexpected and learn to handle things with calmness and professionalism.

The following tips may prove helpful when rendering testimony either at deposition or trial:

- Dress professionally, neatly and conservatively.
- Stand upright when walking to the witness stand and being sworn in.
- While seated at the witness stand, hold your hands lightly together in your lap. Avoid putting your hands to your face. Try to appear at ease. Do not fiddle with pens or ruffle papers.
- Avoid any mannerisms which the jury might interpret as signs of nervousness or falsity.

- Speak clearly and at a pace that will allow the court reporter to get every word.
- Do not be intimidated by opposing attorneys.
- Avoid memorizing your testimony.
- Be serious both on and off the witness stand.
- If you meet other handwriting examiners at court, do not talk with them about the matter at hand. Do not talk about the case in the hallway or restroom. Never speak with opposing parties, attorneys or jurors.
- If you should recognize one of the jurors, bring it to your attorney's attention at the first opportune moment.
- Where possible, talk toward the jurors. Speak to them frankly as if addressing a friend or neighbor. Use the opportunity to educate them about handwriting, something everyone can relate to.
- Listen carefully to all questions, remembering that no matter how seemingly congenial, opposing counsel is out to destroy the effectiveness of your testimony.
- Do not interrupt. Always allow a question to be completed before attempting to answer.
- If you do not know the answer to a question, admit that you do not know.
- If you answer a question incorrectly, correct it immediately.
- Explain your answers when it seems important to do so, rather than just saying yes or no. However, answer only the question asked and do not volunteer information.
- Be cautious of repeated questions on the very same point. The opposition may be trying to get you to contradict yourself by stating a different answer.
- Do not overuse intensifiers like "always," "extremely" or "very."
- Be cautious of questions that include "absolutely" or "positively." Remember that absolute is forever without exception.
- Consider how your testimony will appear in the court record. Refer to documents and exhibits by name or number and be certain that it is clear exactly what you are referring to when you are describing anything in your charts. Nodding, pointing or gesturing cannot be captured by the court reporter.
- Avoid ambiguous remarks such as "I think," "I believe" or "May-

be" which may cause doubt about your conclusions.

- If asked for an estimate, do so as closely as possible but stress that your answer is an estimate. Never trap yourself into giving percentages of opinion such as "I'm 90 percent certain."
- When asked "Will you explain?" or "Why?" consider the door open to clarify yourself.
- Remain polite and professional, even under the most intense cross-examination. At all times avoid appearing arrogant or invincible.
- Never seem defensive during cross-examination.
- If the judge interrupts or if counsel makes an objection, stop talking until it is appropriate to continue.
- Do not be afraid to ask if you may refer to your notes, keeping in mind that opposing counsel may then ask to see those notes.
- Avoid the use of technical language as much as possible. When technical terms are used, explain them so that the jury understands everything you have to say.
- Always clear demonstrative materials with counsel prior to trial.
- Charts used for demonstration must be neat, clear and large enough for every juror to see. If allowed by the court, you may distribute copies of demonstrative materials to jurors, preferably one for every other juror so that if anyone has questions the person next to him will hopefully be able to explain or point out what is being discussed.
- Do not indicate any conclusions on charts or comparison exhibits or they may be disallowed by the court.
- Use highlighting or arrows for emphasis, but avoid making charts overly busy. Simple is always more conducive to understanding, especially to the layperson.
- Use headings that clearly designate what is questioned and what is known.
- If items are enlarged, everything must be enlarged to the same percentage and labeled as such.
- Be sure to prepare enough copies of any comparison charts for all parties. Usually this includes one set for each attorney, one for the judge, one for the court record and one for the examiner's own use. For good measure, an extra set should be prepared.

19. The Business of Handwriting Examination

Client Communications

The initial contact with a prospective client will likely leave a lasting impression. It goes without saying that it should therefore be conducted with professionalism.

In most cases the prospect will inquire as to qualifications and fees. In fact, often the first question, even before providing information about what is at issue, is What do you charge?

Before divulging his fee schedule the examiner should politely question the prospect about the document or handwriting in question so as to elicit pertinent information, such as:

- Is a signature or a larger body of writing involved?
- What are the alleged circumstances surrounding the writing or signing?
- When was the document allegedly signed?
- Is the original document available, or only photocopies?
- If an anonymous writing, how and when was the writing received, and is there a suspect?
- What comparison material is available?

Information regarding comparison material is particularly important, especially with regard to amount, type and date. Most people with handwriting related concerns do not understand the significance of exemplars. Many are under the impression that only one comparison signature is required, or that handprinting can be compared to handwriting, or that a signature dated 1969 can be successfully compared to signatures written in 2005.

It is of course the responsibility of the examiner to educate the potential client as to what is required for the examination, as well as any possible limitations of the exam based on what is reportedly available. Even when the potential client is an attorney it may be necessary to explain these matters, in addition to the likely need to qualify an opinion if no original document is available. The examiner may need to guide the client as to where to find additional exemplars. (Several other document examination texts furnish extensive lists of possible handwriting sources.)

In order to avoid any conflicts of interest, at the initial contact the examiner should query the person as to names of key players. If the caller is not an attorney, he or she should be asked if they are represented by counsel, in which case it will probably be advantageous to speak directly with the attorney. By doing so the examiner will glean information about trial dates and any upcoming deadlines. Also, the attorney will likely explain the matter in a more concise, less emotionally-charged way. Frequently clients have an urge to divulge entirely too much information or feel the need to use the examiner as a sounding board for things that do not relate directly to the handwriting matter.

When speaking with attorneys about cases, potential conflicts should be explored and the examiner should ask who is opposing counsel, what is the anticipated trial date and are there any deadlines? Usually an attorney will query the examiner about qualifications and whether he or she has testified in court. He will often ask for a copy of the expert's curriculum vitae; if not, the examiner should offer to provide it by fax or mail.

Fees are of course an important part of the initial discussion. It is recommended that information about the matter be obtained from the prospective client first, which will allow the prospect to become more comfortable with the examiner before the sometimes touchy issue of money is tackled. He or she will likely be "sold" more easily in this fashion and will be less apt to shop around for other examiners. If the examiner's fees are calculated on an hourly basis, he can supply a ballpark estimate, stressing that charges vary from case to case depending on how complicated and time-consuming they are. The client should be provided with a fee schedule which clearly differentiates between ordinary lab and examination fees as opposed to fees for rendering testimony.

The examiner would be wise to keep notes about the initial interview by using a form such as that furnished here. This will serve as a later reminder should the prospect indicate a desire to "think about it" for awhile. This can also be used to keep tabs on what documentation has been reviewed, how it was received and returned, and whether originals or copies were examined.

It is also recommended that an engagement letter or letter of agreement be written once the client has decided to retain the examiner. At-

CLIENT INTAKE FORM

Client / Attorney ______________________________

Address ______________________________

____

Phone ______________ **Fax** ______________

Case Name ______________________________

Date of First Contact by Client ______________

Engagement Letter Sent ________ ❑ Fax ❑ Mail Returned ________
(date) *(date)*

Trial Date: ______________ Estimated Hours ______________

CV Sent ________ ❑ Fax ❑ Mail Referred by ______________
(date)

Documents

Received________	Returned ________	**Report**:
❑ UPS	❑ UPS	❑ Verbal ________
❑ US Mail	❑ US Mail	*(date)*
❑ Hand Delivered / Pickup	❑ Hand Delivered / Pickup	❑ Written ________
❑ Federal Express	❑ Federal Express	*(date)*
❑ Courier	❑ Courier	
❑ Other	❑ Other	

Nature of Question / Assignment

____

____

Documents in Question

How Many ______ Are originals available? ❑ Yes ❑ No

____

____

Standards

How Many ______ Are originals available? ❑ Yes ❑ No

____

____

Fig. 19.1—Client intake form

torneys are especially receptive to letters of agreement which spell out what is expected from both examiner and client and serve as a protection to both. The agreement letter should also clearly indicate the examiner's fees, both for general examination and rendering testimony.

Curriculum Vitae

One of the first questions the examiner is likely to be asked when contacted by prospective clients (especially attorneys) is, *What are your qualifications?* Given the varied background and training of handwriting examiners, this is an especially valid question. After all, clients deserve to know they're hiring someone competent.

Aside from a verbal answer, a copy of the expert's curriculum vitae (or CV) can be provided. The CV might also be posted on one's website for ease of access by potential and existing clients.

Freely translated from Latin, curriculum vitae means the course or flow of life. It is a concise summation of training, experience and qualifications which will help convince prospective clients of the examiner's capabilities.

As potential clients are often busy people, the more straightforward the CV, the better (without, of course, failing to mention any pertinent credentials).

The expert's CV, along with website, letterhead and business card, constitutes the face that is shown to the business world. The examiner should design the CV to be as professional and polished as possible.

While a résumé is a one or two page summary of one's skills, experience and education, the general purpose of which is to secure employment, a curriculum vitae is generally a longer, more detailed synopsis of educational and academic backgrounds, handwriting and document examination experience, research, publications, awards, honors, affiliations and other professional details.

The CV must be an accurate, up-to-date reflection of the expert's background and training. It should be remembered that it will be subject to scrutiny by one's own client as well as opposing attorneys. All of the facts and details listed should be checked and double checked, as they must be verifiable in court or at deposition. One incorrect entry, if discovered by the opposition, might lead to impeachment on the witness stand.

In general terms a curriculum vitae is used primarily when applying for international, academic, scientific or research positions or when applying for fellowships or grants. Specifically, in the handwriting examination profession the CV is used to evidence one's qualifications, either to prospective clients or to accompany formal document examination reports. When scheduled for depositions, the examiner will likely be asked to bring a copy of his most currently updated CV, and when appearing in court it should also be handy.

How to write a CV

Start by making a list of all background information, then organize it into the categories suggested below. In the early stages of the document or handwriting examiner's career it may seem there are few qualifications to offer, but once skills and assets are listed, one's competence soon becomes evident.

When preparing an effective curriculum vitae, be certain to cover the Five Cs:

1. *Clear*—The CV must be well organized and logical. It should follow a sound and easily understood organizational plan. There can be no confusion concerning any entry. Everything must flow sensibly and in a clearly readable fashion.
2. *Concise*—Stick to what is relevant and necessary. Use phrases rather than complete sentences. Be certain the CV is not "padded" because you may be called upon to explain yourself. Be sure there are no double entries.
3. *Complete*—The CV should include everything needed to evidence your skill level.
4. *Consistent*—Establish a consistent graphic hierarchy so that typeface for equivalent categories of information is the same. Do not mix fonts and styles, make certain all sequences are in proper chronological order, and there is an appearance of organization.
5. *Current*—The CV should be updated frequently as additional experience and training are acquired. Newly gained training such as that offered at document examination conferences will show that the examiner is participating in ongoing education and keeping abreast of new developments in the field.

One's CV should include the following:

- Name and contact information, including current address, phone number, e-mail address and web page address
- Information regarding document examination training (name & location of school, years attended, date of certification)

- Professional experience
- Publications (title, full authorship, journal, date)
- Specialties (ink examination, medical related cases, familiarity with antique documents)
- Record of courtroom testimony. In some jurisdictions experts are required to reveal courtroom history and, in any case, will likely be asked about it.
- Memberships in professional document examination or handwriting organizations
- Areas of research, including a brief description and scope of any research projects
- Presentations (title, full authorship, conference name and location, date)
- References or a client list

What not to include in a CV is also important. There should be no personal information. It is strictly business. The court does not care—or should not—about age, birthplace or marital status.

If the examiner performs graphological services as well as forensic handwriting examination, it is recommended that credentials related to that discipline not be included on the forensic examiner's CV. If so, they will likely be grilled by opposing counsel about the unreliable or unscientific nature of graphology in an attempt to discredit their testimony. (For ways to deal with cross-examination related to graphology, see Chapter 18.)

Additional tips for writing a curriculum vitae are as follows:

- Design your CV so that your strongest qualifications will stand out during a quick review, but with enough detail so that it can stand up to a more careful reading.
- Be sure the CV is easy to read with clean, simple lines and reasonable use of white space on the page.
- Artistic CVs are unacceptable. This is not the time to be cute or pretty. Keep it businesslike and simple but factual.
- Use light-colored (preferably white and definitely not colored) quality paper in standard 8½ x 11 or A4 size.
- Print only on one side of the paper if there is more than one page.
- Use a readable font size. The standard size is 12 point. Do not use

smaller than 10 point or larger than 14 point, although name and contact information may be larger, if desired.

- The examiner's name should be the first readable item. It should appear on its own line.
- Phone number should also be on its own line.
- Use formatting such as boldface, underline, and italics sparingly. Do not use two special formats in one phrase.
- Use common headings such as Certifications, Education, Experience, Accomplishments, Summary of Qualifications, Professional Affiliations, Publications, Honors, References.
- Avoid jargon and acronyms specific to the handwriting and document examination field and, instead, use terms likely to be clearly understood by the general public.
- Avoid graphics, shading or reverses (white letters on a black background).
- Avoid vertical or horizontal lines as well as boxes.
- Avoid using a type that is too light, or copies that are of low quality.

Records Management

An effective filing system is a must in the handwriting examination arena. It is pertinent that the examiner be able to manage and quickly locate both current and past case files.

It is not uncommon for a dormant case to resurface after an extended period of time, sometimes years after the initial work was accomplished. By then the examiner will possibly have forgotten the details of the matter or the names of the players in the case. Or the attorney initially handling the matter may have been replaced.

Therefore, in addition to one's physical filing cabinet, a computerized cross-referenced system is in order. Numerous file management software programs are available and it is the examiner's choice as to which is more preferable. A spreadsheet program is an excellent tool in this regard.

Alternatively, a simple system can be devised using any word processing program that has a search feature and the capacity for generating tables. A table is created with column headings such as case name, players' names, court filing number and name of attorney handling the case. A column for general comments might also be included. Then, when a case comes back to light several years later, the examiner can search the file management document for identifiers which will quickly direct him or her to the location of the actual file.

Nowadays most handwriting and document examiners utilize digital imaging to assist in the examination of cases and creating comparison charts and demonstrative evidence. Scanning case documentation allows for a paperless filing system where both text and images can be stored and retrieved as necessary.

Today the standard format for digitized documents is PDF which is accessible and readable across all computer platforms. Once an entire document has been scanned as a PDF image and placed into a designated computer folder, it can be viewed on screen at various magnifications. Another advantage is the output of original quality copies every time a document is digitally reproduced.

Signatures or other portions of the document that are being examined can be copied from the original PDF image, enlarged to a chosen percentage, and placed into a new comparison document where questioned material is aligned with known. This then can be reviewed on the computer or in printed form.

Additionally, by using image editing software, the examiner can digitally erase any superfluous material surrounding or partially obliterating the writing to facilitate the comparison process. This helps to eliminate anything that might prove distracting to clients or attorneys whose less-trained eyes will later review the comparison charts. (The examiner must not, however, digitally alter the signature or handwriting itself, as that would constitute tampering with evidence. There will likely be questions under cross-examination about any computerized handling of the material. The examiner may use computer software to enhance handwriting for better viewing, such as changing the brightness and contrast of images, but the writing itself cannot be altered in any way. A safe way to handle this is to include in all charts and reports a copy of the original signature before any enhancements were made.)

As they are scanned and stored in the computer, the questioned and known material are of course identified by number. And, as individual signatures or portions of writing are copied from the original digitized file, they also should be identified and saved, perhaps in a subfolder created just for that purpose.

Any notes or worksheets created during the examination can also be carefully identified and saved in the computerized case folder.

This paperless approach obviously eliminates physical storage space, allows for quick searching and access to files and, if carefully planned and maintained, helps eliminate misfiling. It is highly recommended that backups of computerized files be made, preferably one set to keep in one's office and another to be kept off-site in case of disaster such as flood or fire.

The purpose of this book has been to offer useful information pertaining to forensic handwriting examination. As suggested throughout the text, writing identification cannot be reduced to simply matching the strokes of one script and another. The examiner must scrutinize the entire writing and consider the possible influence of internal and external factors on the material in question. It is sometimes a daunting task, even for the seasoned analyst. However, following the book's techniques, procedures and suggestions will help to ensure successful examination results, thereby enhancing the expert's professional image in the handwriting examination arena.

Index

www.ingramcontent.com/pod-product-compliance
Lightning Source LLC
LaVergne TN
LVHW052316200926
848481LV00002B/577